And yet, with every
trip I collect new mementos . . . And all who fish
for bass across the land collect them too.
They are the images from first light to last and
from first fish to last.

First light beckons for that first cast of the day. North Fork of the Shenandoah River, Virginia, by Lionel Atwill.

BASS
FISHING

T hundering down the lake, high-performance rigs skim the surface carrying fishermen to distant parts and saving precious fishing time. It's a game of "Beat the Clock," where 60 miles per hour is standard—enough to squeeze the tears past your temples.

Grand Lake, Oklahoma (above), by Lionel Atwill. Priest Reservoir, Tennessee (left), by Don Wirth.

Anglers emerge from a hidden creek. Obey River, Tennessee, by Don Wirth.

BASS FISHING

An American Tradition

WRITTEN BY GEORGE KRAMER
PRODUCED BY McQUISTON & PARTNERS

THUNDER BAY PRESS, SAN DIEGO

To my dad, Woody Kramer, who didn't fish, but took me anyway, and to my wife, Diana, who lets me keep fishing.

When your job description reads "writer of fish stories," you know that you are in special company. People get paid to do this? And yet, without the experiences and associations shared with so many—and without the opportunity—there would be no stories to write. With that in mind, I must acknowledge some of those who made this project possible.

Lending credence to the scientific and historical side of things were Larry Bottroff of the California Department of Fish and Game; Doug Colle, biologist at the University of Florida; Allen Forshage of the Texas Parks and Wildlife Department; Dr. Loren Hill of the University of Oklahoma; Dr. Larry Paulsen of the University of Nevada at Las Vegas; and Doug Hannon, Florida's "Bass Professor."

Additionally, the scope of these stories would have been narrow, indeed, without the insights and perspectives of Fenwick's David Myers; Florida outdoor writer Tim Tucker; and my personal fly-fishing tutor and program manager for the San Diego City Lakes, Jim Brown.

Likewise I am grateful to every bass fisherman I ever shared a boat or a tale with. But in this particular effort, I must thankfully name-drop some of those professional fishermen—Rich Tauber, Rick Clunn, Gary Klein, and Denny Brauer—who let me share a few tournament moments.

Then, of course, there is Thunder Bay Press, without which there would be no *Bass Fishing: An American Tradition*. I'm indebted to them for giving me the chance to write this book, and to McQuiston & Partners for teaching this writer how to communicate,

and to Robin Witkin for saying "Call me anytime you need help," and then for being there—every time.

And finally, to my friends Rich Holland and Mike Jones, and all the rest who lent support on those dark days when the words wouldn't come—you saved my pork rind.

—George Kramer

Copyright 1990 by Thunder Bay Press. All rights reserved. No part of this book may be reproduced in any form without written permission from the publisher.

Library of Congress Cataloging-in-Publication Data:
Kramer, George, 1947-
    Bass Fishing: an American tradition/by
        George Kramer. p.   cm.
    Includes bibliographical references.
    1. Bass fishing—United States.
I. Title.
SH681.K73 1990   799.1'758—dc20   90-34346 CIP

ISBN 0-934429-76-6
10 9 8 7 6 5 4 3 2 1

Photo Credits
Front cover: Lake Chickamauga, Tennessee by Monte Burch
Back cover: Sommerville Reservoir, Texas by Willard Clay
Frontispiece: Lake Hodges, California by Lionel Atwill

Printed in Japan by Dai Nippon Printing Co., Ltd.

Published by Thunder Bay Press
5880 Oberlin Drive
San Diego, CA 92121

CONTENTS

Day's end at Lake Wright Patman, Texas, by Willard Clay.

Introduction
HEADING UP FOR BASS

I t was the only real tackle shop in town, before the chain stores moved in and the owner retired. But the old brick building had tradition and, like its contents, it seemed to link the enthusiasm of a kid with the savvy of those wiley old veterans hanging around the boathouse. Indeed, it was a place of discovery, if only for a few formative years, and it was there that I found them. The label said "Rubber Worms," though, of course, they were made of plastic. Slick with anise oil, they squirmed through my fingers at the bottom of the apothecary jar. Some were black, some red, while still others were true to the natural earth tones. At a nickel a worm, I was careful to dig through the slippery gob, looking for the straightest and the truest.

"I'm heading up for bass," I told the owner of the shop.

At home, I opened the little brown sack spotted with oil stains. The pungent licorice scent remained, as did the enthusiasm for making my own lures. With beads pirated from Mom's jewelry box, and a spool of nylon line, I rigged tandem hooks on each of the dozen worms I'd bought. The plastic was tough and difficult to penetrate, and the knots and harnesses were crude. But trimmed with pearl or fluorescent pink beads, the lures looked every bit as good to me as those under the glass countertop in the tackle shop. Holding one up to the light, I just knew it was going to catch fish.

Within a week, a willing largemouth proved

the point when it bolted from beneath a mat of floating debris and gaffed itself on my gangly rig. With both hooks in its maw, the bass could run but it couldn't hide, and after a few choice moments, the fish was mine. Looking at the prize today (I traced the 16-incher and stained its silhouette on a piece of wood), I'd say it weighed maybe a couple of pounds. Yet, back then on the dock, a limit-carrying veteran spotted my one and only fish and pronounced, "Son, that's the bass of the day!"

More than 20 years later, in the best American tradition, I find "heading up for bass" as special as ever, kind of like my wife, Diana. For all our familiarity, there are still those little encounters and surprises for both of us. Those bass never know which of the latest gadgetry or lures I'll bring along, and I never know—for certain—if weather or whim will discourage or encourage them on a given day. (It's a lot like my wife in that regard.)

And yet, with every trip I collect new mementos, though few are stained in wood or mounted on scrapbook pages. And all who fish for bass across the land collect them too. They are the images from first light to last and from first fish to last. And we'd share them in a minute. Sure, a few have extra zest, like the anise oil.

Some recall particular triumphs, often preserved in snapshots and clippings, while others we tend to hide, at least until the time we're ready to laugh about them. Daybreaks, canebrakes, heartbreaks, muggy nights, and foggy mornings. A hundred things that worked, and a thousand more that should have. That's bass fishing.

Of course, Ol' *Micropterus* (the black bass genus) should take a lot of credit for the tradition. The largemouth, the smallmouth, the spotted bass, and several lesser varieties have *earned* the title of America's "most popular game fish." And they did so by scoring well in several categories. Certainly they rate highly with regard to *availability*. Following more than a century of introductions into waters outside their original range, largemouth bass are readily found throughout the continental United States, and smallmouth, to a lesser degree, enjoy successful pockets from coast to coast. Supplementing these species are the spotted bass and, in narrower ranges of the Southeast and the Southwest, such varieties as the Suwannee, redeye, Guadalupe, and the shoal bass—*Micropterus* of a different color.

Black bass also receive high marks for their *willingness*. True, there are times when each of these larger members of the sunfish family will challenge—even vex—the most skilled angler. Still, there's no denying their catchability is a positive attribute. When you consider that bass will respond to a range of lures that varies from an innocuous plastic worm to a prop-driven "buzz-bait" with all the subtlety of a paddle-wheeler, you get the feeling these fish are unique opportunists. And yet, bass also have their moments of selectivity when only an item of natural forage, such as a crawfish, shiner, or leech, will draw their attention.

When you finally do get its attention and the fish strikes, you can expect a battle. Black bass are *game*. A largemouth of any consequence is likely to bolt for the nearest tangle of weeds or other cover, straining your tackle and especially your line. In shallow water, it deliberately takes to the air, usually breaking the surface in order to shake its head and toss the hook. But hooked in deep water, a big one often hesitates during a run, again shaking its head and changing directions, sending shudders up the line.

The smallmouth is quicker. It commits suddenly, whether in a river, a craggy natural lake, or a deep impoundment. And when it feels the hook, it darts away until it meets tension on the line, then it explodes as if jettisoned into the air. But what stamina! This leaner bass has enough pluck to make several such jumps and never fails to impress a captor—or a would-be one.

The spotted bass, bless its heart, is a healthy compromise of the aforementioned species. Perhaps a bit too susceptible to live bait, nonetheless, the "spot" is a true slugger, willing to stay down deep, making bull-like rushes while it attempts to retreat to a rocky outcropping. True, it will take a topwater bait and even jump with abandon on occasion, but its usual fight plan is to keep as much water as possible between it and the fisherman—and it does this very well, thank you.

There was a time when I might have added *palatability* to the list of black bass attributes. There is, however, a new awareness that these fish are even more valuable as a recyclable commodity—a sport fish to enjoy again and again—through catch and release. There's no question that bass were first sought as a food fish, and they still are in waterways where they are plentiful. But a bass is just as enjoyable on the end of a line as it would be fried in olive oil and served with Cajun potatoes.

Nearly as savory as bass on a platter are the tasty stories of the development of the sport of bass fishing. While recognition of the bass and native methods for catching them date back to the 1770s, the real innovations in tackle began in the early 1800s with the "Kentucky reel," the first precision baitcasting reel, featuring a near three-to-one retrieve speed. This was also one of

15

the first reels to produce a line-tangling backlash, which then took the tackle industry more than 160 years to eradicate. Still, many of us say that it hasn't been remedied at all.

Certainly spinning reels, popularized after World War II, eliminated a lot of tangled lines and made all fishing easier. Such equipment made casting ultralight lures possible and was appropriate to the clearer waterways where thin monofilament lines were needed to fool the wary smallmouth. But the trend-setting bassin' men of the Southeast established baitcasting gear, heavy line, and stiff rods as the tools of their trade. And so it went during the bass boom of the 1960s and 1970s when such equipment seemed well suited to the largemouth that dwelt in the snag-infested waters of the region. It wasn't until the 1980s that the fierce competition in bass tournaments forced many anglers to rediscover spinning gear in order to finesse more strikes.

On a parallel course, but without the fanfare, fly-fishing for bass is also a part of the bass-fishing heritage.

A game of solitude, it relies on the timeless techniques developed in the British Isles. Indeed, the "single-action" fly reel, with its one-to-one retrieve ratio, has hardly changed since the days of Plymouth Rock. Today, bass-fishing flyrodders are becoming more prevalent but, despite their artful efficiency, fly-fishing Puritans remain in the minority.

And therein is a certain irony of modern bass fishing. Efficiency is the watchword of the professional bass angler. Efficiency marks the progression of the sport. Yet, instead of the practiced hand with the long rod and the popping bug or streamer, bass-fishing efficiency is usually associated with high-speed reels, surgical-quality hooks, and sleek fishing craft mounted with multiple depth finders. Bass boats are the symbol of technological fishing, but a push-pole in a wooden johnboat will mark the bottom of a slough as well as sonar. And maybe there is no irony at all. Just room for divergent methods, divergent pleasures, and divergent opinions about bass fishing—an American tradition.

Private pond near Ocala, Florida, by Lionel Atwill.

A consistent water flow, especially in the heat of summer, and a forage base of crawfish and assorted chubs make a surprise largemouth haven. That bass fishermen are scarce in these parts doesn't hurt.

There's something in the morning mist that says "today is going to be special." Those steamy pockets on the water provide a certain sanctuary where the bass fisherman is cloistered in the privacy of his expectations.

Pomme de Terre Lake, Missouri (above), by Monte Burch.
Saint Croix River, Wisconsin (right), by Tom Till.

Wolf Lake, Wisconsin, by Willard Clay.

Reading the water is a game the bass fisherman constantly plays. In the shallow pond, he looks for vegetation like these sparse lily pads that might signal a bottom contour or composition change that might encourage the presence of fish in the area.

Lake Daingerfield, Texas, by Willard Clay.

Water lilies and largemouths go together like salt and pepper, but where under the mass of umbrellas are they hiding? A few inches below an opening in the pads could sit the biggest bass in the lake—if only you make the right cast.

File under: Daybreaks, unforgettable. Gull Lake, Minnesota, by Wade Bourne.

LIVE BAIT! CRAWDADS, SHINERS, & SUCH

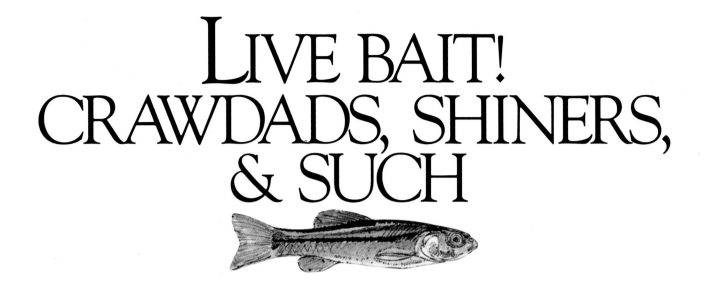

P
ut on a crawdad. Eat some Fritos. And shut up!"

Not exactly the consolation I was seeking on this trophy bass hunt gone awry, but then maybe that's part of the challenge. Bob Holcomb was a veteran live-bait fisherman and, as you can tell, not one to mince words. In retrospect, I figure he'd probably waded through many of the same anxieties that now had me by the throat, but that didn't make me feel any better. The morning had not been pleasant.

After several weeks of following the fish movements and charting "new" structures, we had carefully established a plan that would grant us access to two ideal rock piles at the same time. Armed with

plastic pans crowded with the crawfish we had worked all night to collect, I knew that heavy stringers were only hours away. First off from the dock, we directed the wooden rental boat to the main basin of the little reservoir, barely a half-mile trip. Searching for landmarks on the shore and eyeing the spokes of light on the fish-finder, we dropped a marker buoy on the edge of a submerged peak, made another looping pass with the boat, and set the anchors a hundred feet in either direction. We unpacked our beach chairs and untangled our rods, and then looked over our position with a certain smugness. Not only had we reached the area first, but our extended scope to each anchor would allow us to slide forward or back, depending on where the fish were biting best. Logistically, we were perfect. But our plan had a serious flaw. It did not allow for the host of other anglers on the lake that day—or for their similar desires for success.

There are very few secrets on a 125-acre pond. Apparently our isolated rock piles were not so difficult to find after all, and those anglers who had any questions about their location quickly found answers in our Styrofoam buoy, camouflaged with Day-Glo paint, of course. Only free money could have drawn a larger crowd. The first boat to approach did show some restraint. It anchored perhaps a hundred feet away on the opposite side of the rock pile. But seeing two boats in the same area, the next one split the difference, and two others tossed concrete anchors to our right. Within 30 minutes such a flotilla had assembled that it was hard to find our buoy just a short cast away.

Today I smile. But that morning was filled with pain, self-pity, and bitterness. These blips were ruining my fishing trip, yet helplessly I kept casting. Disdain swelled for my fellow anglers and their idle questions: "No. We're not doing a dang thing." "No, we didn't hear about the big one caught last week!" And then I broke. "Hey! You're so close, why don't you get into the boat with us?!"

By midmorning I was finished. Take my rod, take my tackle, just get me back on the highway. I couldn't get a bite on a plastic worm or a nightcrawler, and even our cache of prize crawdads was sulking, hunkered down like a tray of dry radishes. Like McClellan on the Potomac, great plans had gone for naught. Near noon, at the peak of my disgust, I finally sued for peace. "Let's get out of here," I pleaded.

Hesitating only to open the ice chest, Holcomb removed the familiar red-and-orange plastic bag and issued the "Put on a crawdad" command. I hated to disturb the crusty little things, but the day required a bit more commitment, as far as my partner was concerned. I pinched one behind the head before it caught on to the game and laid its larger claw on the narrow wooden gunwale. Pressing firmly at the base of the pincer, I crushed the shell and the crawdad released the entire appendage at the shoulder. Like the lizard's sacrificial tail, Nature gives crawfish an escape clause and fishermen a better way to control their bait. With only half its holding power, the craw would be easier to maneuver along the bottom and was less likely to cling to underwater limbs. With a tiny #6 through the telson, I lobbed the unweighted bait some 30 feet in front, put the rod between my legs, and opened the bag in silence.

Settling into the chair's vinyl straps and feeling the metal frame wince, I spent the next few minutes in therapeutic crunching. Perhaps it was the salt satisfying a need in the heat, or maybe it was just the bulk filling an empty spot. Whatever the case, it was working. Three or four handfuls later, I was almost ready. Wiping the salt and yellow grit on my shirt, I lifted the rod to pick up slack, turned the handle a few times, and reopened the bail. I fingered the line in my left hand and began knitting a pile of loops on the deck in front of me. And since it is necessary to let a bass run with the bait, the loose line and open bail posed no threat of a missed strike.

And there was a strike. Muted as it was, the light kicking on the line meant the one-armed crawfish was fleeing for its life. I dropped the line and watched it lift off the planks and spin out through the guide. Then it stopped as the bass of a lifetime crushed the crawfish's carapace like a handful of corn chips. Turning the bait in its mouth in order to swallow it tail-first, the fish moved off again, clearly unaware of the circumstances.

What happened next was a combination of fishing mechanics and old-fashioned luck. Lifting the rod, I set on the fish, trying to keep it from tearing out the hook. But this bass didn't even shrug as it moved away. I thought, "All right! Break the ice!" But moments later,

as I made no progress at all, another thought surfaced: "Bob, this feels like a good fish."

"Bob. This feels like the fish we've been looking for."

"Bobbb!"

Even though I saw the move coming and sunk the rod to the grips, the fish broke through the surface, pausing on the taut line and loaded fiber glass. There it was, just for an instant, an eye and a mouth. And back down it went, pulling drag and wiping a dozen years of fishing experience from my consciousness. I blanked out; I admit it. Reacting to the fish, Holcomb counseled me to back off on the drag, but I stared at the reel and didn't have the faintest idea which way to loosen it. A limber rod surely saved me. After making one last rush for the forward anchor, the tired fish settled into the mesh and Holcomb lifted it aboard.

It was near dark when we finally pulled the anchor—the stringer laden and the bait tray almost empty. By design, the scale on the dock marked pounds and ounces, hardly enough to measure this weighty trip. But for a single bass—my trophy—the needle spun, quivering to a stop a few ticks from the 11-pound mark. And a crawdad made it all possible.

Of course, it's not all that surprising. Live bait, such as the widely distributed crawfish, often account for

25

big bass. Florida's Doug Hannon, the one called the "Bass Professor" and a fellow with more than 600 ten-pounders (and larger) to his credit, reveals the biological implications of live bait versus artificials. Even though black bass have been caught on everything from french fries to chunks of cut mackerel, they generally "react better to live bait because live bait *reacts* to the predator bass. Before a fish makes a decision to feed, it has to determine that a bait, regardless of its type, is one it wants. When a bass charges up to a crankbait, it is looking for a reaction. It follows along, but if the lure doesn't react to the presence of the bass, it won't strike."

Many live-bait fishermen are more concerned with the bottom line, however. Whether it's leeches in Minnesota, shiners in Florida, crawfish in California, or salamanders and sirens wherever they're found, live bait is big business because fishermen like results. And the only people who are more fanatic about bait use than those who buy theirs at the local marina are those who catch and care for their own. I was one of the latter.

This goes back a way, of course. There were no kids then in the new apartment, no dogs, no birds, only the endless bubbling of the bath-size aquarium in the living room—the residence of a captive largemouth. Three rooms were plenty, daily schedules ran from the swing to the graveyard, and my wife, Diana, was still new and vulnerable too. It was getting toward the weekend, and I had already spent one night wading through a drainage ditch, scooping up netfuls of muck and hoping that my flashlight wouldn't disturb the neighbors. The catch was slim, maybe a couple dozen craws, but they were in good condition, and that was the way I was going to keep them.

Since my place was the last stop on the way to the lake, I became the keeper of the craws. And because it was the warmest part of the year, the bait could not be kept on the patio. Left out in the sun, crawfish shells harden, creating a crusty, unsuitable bait. Likewise, the shallow water that houses them heats up and loses oxygen, suffocating the crawfish and, frankly, creating a soup of indescribable displeasure. And that's why they have air-conditioning, I suppose. In the kitchen I transformed several milk cartons into custom bait containers, each with a flap for easy access. Not only would they hold a dozen baits, they would also fit nicely into an ice chest. And they were cheap. Unfortunately, as my wife later discovered, they weren't all that secure.

We didn't cross paths on the night in question. Diana had left for work about 3:00 in the afternoon, and I did my handiwork several hours later. When she returned home, she didn't investigate the milk cartons, preferring to keep to her routine of settling into bed with a book. Snug in her safe haven, she would fall asleep soon enough. Until then, Agatha Christie would have to keep her company. But something violated the stillness of the apartment. It wasn't the aerators in the other room . . . it sounded more like something scraping on paper. Diana put her book down and listened more closely. There it was again—a faint scraping or scratching. Where was it coming from?

Yesterday's newspaper was tossed about on the carpet next to the nightstand. Was that where it was? And if so, what was down there? Diana peered over the edge of the bed, not sure she wanted to know. Several of the largest crawdads were canvassing the place. Having escaped confinement, the nocturnal critters no doubt were searching for water. The ensuing moments must have been like vintage Lucille Ball. Unwilling to handle the errant crustaceans, Diana tried to herd them onto a single sheet of newsprint. But as soon as two were collected, another would inch away or roll out of reach. It took several tries before she stiff-armed the catch back into the kitchen where she funneled them into an empty carton.

Sleep, of course, was now out of the question as three harmless arthropods had produced a higher heart rate than Ms Christie ever could have. A search party was needed to secure the zone, and Diana was that party. I guess she didn't realize that crawfish could climb a 90-degree dust ruffle. Or drapes. Or that they could reach a cornice box within hours, commanding a view of the entire room.

The best part was the phone call. *"Your things got into my room!"*

It is apparent that proper bait-handling techniques were something we had not discussed early in our marriage, which was an oversight. Considering that crawfish offer such a wide range of availability, both as forage for black bass and as potential live bait, it's difficult to understand how we had not communicated.

Perhaps more significant to fishermen than bait handling is understanding something of the crawfish's life cycle and how it relates to predator–prey interaction in its environment. Crawfish have an exoskeleton; their vulnerable body parts grow and function within the hardened shell. They molt at various times as their body grows, and although molting is a desirable function, it places the crawfish in severe danger from predators for short periods. At the outset of the molting process, a crawfish exudes certain enzymes that soften the carapace (shell), pincers and all. Then, when pliable enough,

27

the animal simply backs out of his "old clothes" and secretes a new body covering that eventually hardens.

Fishermen refer to crawfish passing through the molt as "soft shells" and consider them first-rate as live bait. However, since growth characteristics vary according to the individual, it's difficult to gather many soft shells at one time. Although bait collecting may be random in securing this high-quality bait, wild black bass and other game fish track these helpless creatures by sensing the molting enzymes in the water. What's more, not only are various species of fish on their trail, but other cannibalistic crawfish are as well.

It's no wonder that crawdads exhibit such multiple personalities. Sometimes they cower in the face of reality, while at other times, they steadfastly choose a defensive posture. Finally, there are those occasions when they seem ready to take on the world. These latter two circumstances need to be addressed by the would-be live-bait fisherman, not so much with the smaller craws used for smallmouth or spotted bass, but with the jumbo specimens that relish the sight of an unsure hand reaching into the bait bucket. A crawfish takes it as a personal affront when tender office-worker flesh comes its way. In fact, raising your hand to a crusty adult is as much a mistake as raising your hand at an auction. In either case, you're gonna pay. No wild animal that has risked death a dozen times while growing to adulthood is going to acquiesce while you grab it in a choke hold and stick a piece of steel through its gut.

Body language, then, is the key. Like any trial by fire, picking up a big craw calls for a calm approach and a steady hand, though not necessarily "nerves of steel." However, if you fail to convince the animal of your good intentions, you might need "hands of steel" because a crawdad can draw blood with its pincers. But that is the reality of choosing a bait. You may know what size and what color "dad" you want, but if you can't get it on the end of your line, you're not fishing. The best way to approach any well-endowed (meaning heavily clawed) crawfish is with your hand flat, palm up. The idea is to move closer toward it without exhibiting any threatening arm or body movements. Be deliberate and try to place your hand so that the crawfish can step with all 10 legs right onto your palm. Its first reaction may be to fend you off, or even nip you, but an otherwise unthreatened craw will remain calm.

The next move requires the same sure confidence. However, since you now carry this beastie in your hand, should it become alarmed, it's going to crimp your hide with *both* claws! Take heart, you can do it. Bring your hand up from below and behind the craw and pinch it around the carapace and right behind the shoulders. In essence, your thumb and forefinger surround the thorax like the legs of a bronc rider, and for much the same reason, you don't want to let go. While the craw will reach back with its pincers, it shouldn't be able to get you. If it does, however, you'll have to make some adjustments—perhaps by rereading the preceding paragraphs. Or perhaps by switching to earthworms for bait.

Choosing a live bait, whether it's small bluegills, earthworms, crawfish, or whatever, is often crucial to bass-fishing success. This brings up an important point regarding forage (and bait) for black bass. Dr. Loren Hill, head of the Zoology Department at the University of Oklahoma, contends that bass feed primarily on whatever's available at the time. For instance, sonar tracking has shown that bass movements correlate directly with the distribution of baitfish. Obviously, if there are no indigenous shad or leeches or insect hatches of consequence, then they will not be a part of the food chain.

Nonetheless, in the Sunbelt regions that Dr. Hill has studied, black bass tend to show a preference among live forage when given the opportunity for a selection. Both shiners and shad, two soft-finned fish, tend to be targeted first in laboratory settings. Crawfish are next in line, favored by bigger bass since they provide more calories (actually protein) for the effort that it takes to collar them. Next, the bass will choose frogs and amphibians. Immature salamanders with exposed, blood-laden lamella (gills), however, might even outprovoke a shiner, like a red bikini during spring break. However, according to Dr. Hill, frogs were rarely ever found in the stomach contents of black bass. He reported that, during his entire career, he had never seen a single tadpole that had been devoured by a bass. Finally, among the animals studied, the last on the "preferred menu" are the spiny-ray fishes such as the bluegill, redear, or other sunfish. Thus, knowing the forage preferences of laboratory bass and identifying the types of forage available in a specific waterway are steps toward successful angling. But regardless of the bait selected, the issue is clear. Sometimes, it's gotta be alive.

29

They call it "the wood," those trees, stumps, even fence-posts that stagger to the shore and disappear beneath the surface. They might be cottonwoods in California, willows and ironwood in Texas, or even these cypress and tupelo gum in Illinois, but they're uniquely favored by the largemouth. Finding wood in combination with some aquatic plants is a productive fish-catching pattern.

Lake Weir, Florida (above), by Lionel Atwill. Horseshoe Lake, Illinois (left), by Willard Clay.

Sam Rayburn Reservoir, Texas, by Willard Clay.

Ｉn early spring it's the willows that draw the Texas bass busters to the creek mouths of the legendary Sam Rayburn Reservoir. The big bass move first from the hydrilla beds to the willows, and finally into the shallow buckbrush to make their nests.

Lake Erie, Ohio, by Tom Till.

B ut in the northlands, the smallmouth bass may flourish in more craggy environs such as these on Lake Erie. From Marblehead Light in the distance, summer charter boat captains forget about walleyes and venture to the famed Bass Islands for "jumpers."

—34

Gunsight Butte at Lake Powell, Glen Canyon National Recreation Area, Utah, by Tom Till.

Gee. It ought to look great once they get the landscaping in," said Arkansas cartoonist Cliff Shelby of the desert Southwest. Yet, the Colorado River lakes have thriving black bass fisheries and often host major tournament competition.

Volcanic rock, sparse vegetation, and crystalline waters are a far cry from the lush settings and murky waters of the Southeast, but this is home to bass in the West. Here a pair of tournament fishermen work a shady bank at Lake Mead before the desert sun drives the fish to deep water.

A heartstopper in the hyacinth. Lake Griffin, Florida, by Kitty Pearson-Vincent.

THE FLORIDA HEAVYWEIGHTS

I wonder what the *old* lake record is here?" I often needle as we head out in the morning looking for big bass. Even among the most pensive partners, the question usually draws a smile, or a smirk. But there's more than a burst of bravado that elicits the mock query. After all, at the rate largemouth bass records have tumbled over the last decade or so, the likelihood of one falling today or tomorrow is pretty good. The curious part of the record fish trend is that regardless of the waterway or state in which it occurs, the new record fish will very likely be a *Florida bass.*

The Florida-strain largemouth bass, *Micropterus salmoides floridanus,* esteemed for its exceptional growth rates in its original range throughout Florida and parts of Georgia, has become the talk of the town, so to speak, as it tours the temperate regions of the country. And though the Florida bass first found its way into new areas by migrating through existing river systems, its presence in many other distant locations is due to deliberate introductions by fishery managers. Because of this effort, the Florida bass is providing many new opportunities for trophy-size fish.

Although it was not identified as a separate subspecies of largemouth bass, M. *salmoides,* until 1949, bass anglers already knew that the largest black bass came from the Southeast. Indeed, the longest-standing bass record is the Florida state mark of 20 pounds 2 ounces set back in 1923. Many other huge bass were recorded in this portion of the country, but not until the bass boom years of the 1960s and 1970s was the trophy potential of the Florida large-mouth tapped by other states.

Although Texas is now considered one of the most innovative states because of its waterway-specific management program, back in 1971, it took the enthusiasm, and personal funds, of the late Robert Kemp, Jr., the Texas fisheries director, to get the first Florida fingerlings delivered to the state hatchery in Tyler. Nine years later, the 37-year-old state record for bass was bested by a 14-pound, 1-ounce Florida bass from Lake Monticello. And since that time, virtually every major reservoir record in the state has been held by a Florida bass, topped tenuously in 1986 with a 17-pound 10-ounce fish from Lake Fork.

Because the "new" bass hailed from a unique southeastern environment of year-round temperate conditions, Texas authorities planted the first Floridas in so-called power plant lakes, whose waters were used to cool electric generators. Even during the winter months, these small lakes received artificially heated water, which was thought to maintain a seasonable environment for the imported bass. However, as more fish were released

into other Texas waters, it became clear that the Floridas' temperature tolerances were not so different from the northern or native-strain bass. Today, all the state's largest fish caught have come from unheated lakes.

But Florida bass might never have toured Texas, Arkansas, Mississippi, or Alabama for that matter, had it not been for earlier experimentation in California. As the story goes, former big-league baseball player Ray Boone told friends in San Diego about the big bass he had seen in Florida during spring training. He wondered why California couldn't have those same big fish. Conferring with associates on the San Diego County Fish and Game Commission, Boone rallied support for the idea; and later, assisted by California Department of Fish and Game biologist Orville Ball, the first Floridas were reluctantly brought to California.

Following one unsuccessful attempt to bring fish into the state (parasites were found on the stock), a second group arrived from the Pensacola hatchery on May 20, 1959. These fish were released into a tiny reservoir known as Upper Otay in Chula Vista, while the adjacent reservoir, Lower Otay, a 1,300-acre lake to the south, received the first plants. In short order, virtually every one of the small reservoirs (none over 1,500 surface acres) in the county received the imports.

By 1966 bass identified as Floridas weighing as much as 9 pounds 8 ounces were caught. In 1968 a 15-pound largemouth that would have exceeded the state record was found dead. During the following decade, anglers took turns pummeling the California standard with Florida bass—16 pounds 10 ounces in 1971, 17 pounds 14 ounces in 1972, 20 pounds 15 ounces in 1973, and 21 pounds 3 ounces in 1980—from three different bodies of water!

Obviously, the Florida bass had a unique genetic makeup and an ability to continue to grow throughout its 10- to 15-year life-span. But the strain was curious in other ways. In California waters where Floridas were introduced, statistics showed that the native bass were being caught out at a rate of more than two to one over the Floridas. Despite their apparent aggressive feeding nature, Floridas did not take the hook and line as well. For whatever reasons, they seemed more able to care for themselves in the wild, a point not lost during radio telemetry studies conducted in the mid-1970s. To study their movements, biologist Michael Lembeck fitted several large specimens ranging from 6 to better than 10 pounds with small transmitters. Although his studies

showed that big bass were highly individualistic, they also revealed a clear recognition of "angling pressure" by the fish. One bass, for instance, would retreat to the buoyed "no fishing" area when the lake opened for business. And especially telling was a fish at El Capitan Lake in California that, despite murky waters, seemed to know it was being pursued.

A young Mike Folkestad, now one of the West's premier fishing pros, took part in those exercises: "Mike (Lembeck) would wear the headphones and locate a bass. If we kept our distance, the fish would hold its ground. But as soon as I would make a cast in the direction of the fish, as soon as the bait hit the water, the fish would swim away. We did this several times, and the fish would react (negatively) every time to the worm." It's no wonder these fish could grow to such proportions with that kind of ability to avoid capture.

Yet for all the growth potential of the Florida strain, and despite sightings and rumors of larger specimens both in the United States and Central America, George Perry's world record of 22 pounds 4 ounces is still standing even at the threshold of the 1990s. Despite armies of anglers and technology unheard of over 50 years ago, Perry's bass looms larger than life. Caught on a wooden lure with a metal diving bill in 1932 from Georgia's Montgomery Lake, the bass was weighed but never photographed. There were no financial benefits, no endorsements—the fish was its own reward, feeding a needy family in the depths of the Great Depression.

As the years passed and generations of black bass lived out their lives without surpassing the stature of Perry's fish, the aching question seemed to be: How could his bass grow to be so large when clearly native largemouths have been judged unable to attain such dimensions? Was Perry's fish a fluke? Was Perry's fish real?

The answer may lie in a technique known as electrophoresis (an analysis of proteins in animal tissue), which is considered the most reliable method of identifying Florida bass from its other subspecies. Recently, biologists determined that waters in both Georgia and Alabama show traces of long-existent "intergrading" between the two subspecies. That is, the Florida bass, at the periphery of its natural range, has mixed or crossbred with the native bass for a long time, delivering its genetic magnificence to the progeny. In other words, as postulated by University of Florida biologist Doug Colle, there is little doubt that "Perry's fish was a Florida-strain bass."

So George Perry's tale is a bit more palatable to those who seek but cannot reach the long-standing world record, and the legacy of the Florida bass continues. Still other, far more incredible tales seem to follow the Florida's big-fish heritage across the land. Such is the story of the "second-largest bass" ever taken. Unfolding on San Diego's Lake Miramar, the story involves an employee of the concession stand who made her first solo bass-fishing trip on March 14, 1988 and, in doing so, became an enigma of modern bass fishing. Leaving ticket-selling chores to her husband, Sandy DeFresco climbed into a rental boat and pushed off from the dock. Within 15 minutes, she had hooked, reeled, and, after suffering a backlash on the unfamiliar tackle, finally hand-lined a Florida bass weighing 21 pounds 10 ounces—just 10 ounces shy of the world record.

With her fish instantly heralded as a new California mark, Mrs. DeFresco and her attorney set out to cash in on the catch. Within days she had contact with several major tackle companies. And although the bass was not *the* record, it was enormous, and news of it impacted the entire bass-fishing community. But just one week later, the world was jolted a second time when the taxidermist mounting the huge fish discovered a 2½-pound diver's belt weight in its stomach!

The initial reaction was that this was fraud, pure and simple. But DeFresco's testimony never wavered. What's more, with the shiny lead chunk, a "piece of gristle," as it was described, was also found. Noted California Department of Fish and Game biologist Larry Bottroff suspected that the piece of organic material might have been produced by the bass to act as a buffer against the presence of the foreign material. But 2½ pounds of lead was just too much for most observers to swallow. DeFresco's attorney advised his client not to seek recognition for the fish, wisely sensing the growing controversy.

However, her new attorney went ahead with the case. After months of deliberation, the State of California refused to recognize the fish as a state record. Not wanting to focus blame, the Department of Fish and Game merely determined that the lead was too significant a part of the fish's total weight. The International Game Fish Association, on the other hand, with its strict rules governing the landing of a fish, could not accept the fish in any event because it was hand-lined. Finally, in a move particularly galling to Californians, the respected National Freshwater Fishing Hall of Fame in Hayward, Wisconsin accepted DeFresco's Florida-strain bass of 19 pounds 1 ounce (without the lead) as a 15-pound test line class record.

So the world record remains at bay, as fishermen pursue the genetically marvelous Florida bass. Perhaps it's true, as Dr. Malcolm Stock once stated during the Carter administration, having seen seven presidents come and go since the world record for bass was established in 1932, that "catching a world record bass was at least seven times harder than becoming president of the United States."

B ass are where you find them" is one of those timeless axioms that leave newcomers scratching their heads. Yet there are certain places that just draw you in for a closer look—places that make you want to stop and maybe toss a plastic worm.

Table Rock Lake, Missouri, (above), by Charles J. Farmer.
Dead River Beach State Park, Illinois (right), by Willard Clay.

Lake Mohave, Arizona, by Lionel Atwill.

The *book* on black bass says "rising water, fish shallow." The rock outcropping gives this bank walker a sure vantage point from which to fish this flooded brush. In a manner of speaking, the fish come to the fisherman following the spring runoff and the bass's natural urges for nesting.

Blue Springs, Florida, by Kitty Pearson-Vincent.

Depending on the type of waterway, spawning largemouths look for the shallowest backwaters that provide protective cover for nests. Such areas tend to warm up earlier and may only be accessible by a nimble craft with a shallow draft.

45

46

Montrose Wildlife Area, Missouri, by Monte Burch.

The archetype of the "bass boat" is seen on every waterway from Oregon to Maine, and the reason is its highly functional design. A trolling motor maneuvers it through the thin waters, and a pair of swivel seats lets two fishermen cast in harmony.

Rodman Reservoir, Florida, by Kitty Pearson-Vincent.

Before the development of the high-performance bass boat, the johnboat was the traditional rig for fishing the quiet waters favored by the largemouth. But one thing hasn't changed—the bass fishermen's preference to fish in pairs.

Sunset on Somerville Reservoir, Texas, by Willard Clay.

BENEATH THE MOON & UNDER THE SUN

How hot was it out there?" the fellow with the microphone asked as he hastened along the line of weary fishermen. He and another sweaty soul with a camera strapped to his shoulder were smiling impishly as they picked me out of a group waiting to weigh their day's catch from Nevada's miserly Lake Mead. Drained by the desert sun, and not expecting the attention considering my slender catch, I didn't understand him at first, so he repeated, "How hot *was it* out there?"

"It was so hot . . ." I stammered for an appropriate comparison, "that the plastic worms melted right in their trays."

In downtown Las Vegas, the thermometer flashed 115°F atop the Sahara Hotel. But up on the lake some locals claimed it was another 5 degrees hotter; obviously, they didn't work for the Chamber of Commerce. And yet, the fishermen were there in force—255 men and women from 24 states—baking their respective brains in the good name of bass fishing. And I was amazed to find that after three more days of similar torture, many of the sunburned competitors gladly laid down deposits for yet another opportunity to incinerate the following July!

That next summer and for several ensuing years I reconvened with those anglers, mostly as a reporter but occasionally as an on-the-water observer. Without any prizes on the line for the media, it seemed unnecessary to reexperience the desert as I had each day during the inaugural event in 1981. Indeed, lugging a quart of Gatorade while communing with writers from other parts of the country seemed a more prudent way to cover the contest. It was also an opportunity to gain a perspective on summer bass fishing from those who had endured the weather in other regions. One issue often raised in the pressroom was *humidity*. From Saint Paul, Minnesota to the Saint Johns River in Florida, summers are not only warm, they're uncomfortably "close." For that reason, the discussion went, the "dry" heat of the desert was reputed to be more bearable. That myth was quashed, however, by Florida writer Tim Tucker who declared, "There's no humidity in a microwave either, but it's still hot."

And yet, summer remains a popular time for bass fishing. Warmer weather and water temperatures, depending on the latitude, generally mean that black bass are more active and more willing to strike. Many bass-fishing safaris are scheduled during this period, sometimes under the guise of a family vacation, and anglers head out to places they've only read about—the "boundary waters" of northern Minnesota, the James River in Virginia, or the world-famous San Diego "City Lakes." (Of course, if you live in Duluth or Richmond or if you're stationed at San Diego's Miramar Naval Air Sta-

tion, you might not get away with the vacation ploy, but it's worth a try!)

Even in inviting surroundings, however, too much summer bass fishing tends to lose its savor like a piece of pork rind left parched and dangling on a spoon. As it does with the fatty rind, the sun bakes some of the fun out of the fishing and takes its toll on your gear as well. I once ordered several-dozen hard (plastic) baits for an extended trip to central Arizona. There were Cordell Spots, Norman Rippin' Minnows, and Rebel Pop R's—both solid and plastic foam construction—and I stuffed them into the upper trays of one of those new tackle boxes with the translucent lids. One blistering day fishing was pretty good, especially on the plastic worms, so the tackle box stayed up on deck where I could reach the disposable crawlers. As the sun began to wane, I located some bass chasing shad and decided to switch to a Rippin' Minnow. Unfortunately, the heat of the day had done more than make potato chips out of my ears. Inside the tackle box, in what had become a plastic oven, the sun had swollen every one of the foam plastic lures into polystyrene mutants.

Long summer days on the water are also where I learned the definition of *carcinoma*. The threat of skin cancer was first revealed to bass fishermen at the U.S.

Open tournament at Lake Mead. The staff dermatologist for a sunscreen manufacturer invited all contestants and press observers to submit to a cursory examination of their exposed parts. We formed a single line and the doctor stretched the skin on our forearms and on the backs of our hands. He peered at our noses and tugged at our ears. When he'd finished, his pronouncement was stunning. Over 75 percent of the "study group" had some precancerous growths. Sunscreen sales were brisk.

With such liabilities associated with daytime summer fishing, some alternative to the dawn-to-dusk routine is certainly needed. Even discounting the extreme conditions associated with the desert, there has to be something more pleasant than muggy, breathless days or the sensation of wearing someone else's swampy gym shirt. For a curious few, there is—bass fishing after-hours.

Those who ply the waters after sunset make up a bass-fishing subculture. You may not even notice them; they're the ones whose boats arrive as you pull out in the afternoon. You may even see them on the highway, appropriately going the opposite way. Indeed, they may even exist in your own neighborhood, rolling out of their driveways just as you begin to forage in the kitchen. They know the nocturnal nature of the black bass during the summer, and they know where the action is.

In certain circles, for instance, the bass-fishing nightlife displays some of the trappings of its social counterpart—a night on the town. Once lighted by black lights mounted on the deck, night fishermen using fluorescent line sent streaking casts through the night air. From across a cove the boat was nearly invisible, but the line, absorbing energy from the purple glow, clung to the darkened rod on the back cast and then flew parallel over the water as the fisherman followed through. Few sights in bass fishing were as vivid or as fleeting. Fleeting because lighted line dims as it stretches beyond the range of the black light. And because most nighttime anglers no longer believe it is necessary to "see" every strike (a telltale twitch in the glowing line that determines when a bass has taken the bait). The reduced sale of fluorescent lines evidences this change of heart, and today we see the darker side of bass fishing.

Lights of any kind are rarely used in actual night-fishing situations since a sudden or intense beam on the water will usually spook the bass. Thus a spotlight is only used to illuminate familiar landmarks—or hazards—while in transit. Launching before sunset improves the chances of safe navigation because it gives you one final opportunity to familiarize yourself with the surroundings. Still, I submit, our memories for even the

51

most distinctive features are sometimes lacking.

I remember an outing when my partner justified a forgotten spotlight bulb with "Heck, it's a small lake, we won't need it." But the fish were particularly devious that night. They tempted us with occasional bites, steadily drawing us well down the winding river arm. For hours we tried the major points on both sides of the lake, trying to find a school of feeding fish, until it became perfectly clear that we couldn't see where we were going or where we'd been. Turning into the wind that rippled the surface of the water, we tried to find our way, looking for a light or promontory that might mark the course back to our truck and trailer. Unfortunately, one point was indistinguishable from any other, and every light drew us in where we intruded on fishermen who weren't lost. It was well after midnight when we found the main launch ramp. I could have shot my partner, but I couldn't see him.

Hey, night fishing is like that. "You find out if you've got your stuff together," one veteran told me. The cool air is invigorating, and there is a certain solitude, even with your fishing partner only a few feet away. Out on the water there is also a feeling of isolation; yet sound carries well—like the splash of a bass being landed in another boat or the muffled voices of fellow anglers.

"You get that one on a Gatortail, Ronnie?"

"Yeah. Black with a firetail."

"You got summore?"

"In my satchel. Should be right on top."

"Where's it at? I don't see it."

"It's right there, ain't it? Should be on the ice—. Jack, where's the dang ice chest? Jack!"

"Ronnie . . . I think I left 'em back on the dock."

Of course, having it "together" reflects on every part of night fishing. Casting is certainly an adventure. After dark, bass are usually shallow and that means a lot of casting toward the bank. If you're lucky, the shoreline is dotted with docks and boathouses marked with security lights. But if it isn't, you aim toward the same kinds of cover you would fish during the day—rocky points, stumps, or flooded timber. Using "muscle memory" from years of practice, you figure it's no problem winging a cast and pinching down on the spool at the moment you expect the lure to touch down.

At night, however, this infallible system is compromised. The rod loads up, the bait swings forward, and the spool spins. But you can't track the lure through the air, so you don't thumb the spool in time, and your bait lands 3 feet long in a treetop. The lure stops all right, but the spool doesn't. The line fluffs up, tangling in itself and rendering the reel unserviceable for the rest of the night. Now, figuring that the average angler might get one backlash in 20 casts in the dark, how many rods must he carry to fish the entire evening?

But casting is only one part of the night-fishing scene. Tying knots is equally crucial and just as exasperating. No matter how many outfits you bring aboard, you're going to have to change lures or retie a hook sometime. Whether you tie a Uni, or a Palomar, or an improved clinch, the situation is the same. Every knot requires putting an invisible piece of monofilament line through the suddenly microscopic eye of the hook. And in the depths of a moonless night, quite frankly, you'll discover that it can't be done. That is, unless you incorporate some kind of night-light.

I always figured a miner's helmet would be ideal. With the light switched on, you could focus on what you were doing and then turn it off so that your eyes would stay adjusted to the darkness. It would also serve as protection against flying lures—the ones you try to dislodge from the treetops that always seem to snap back at your head. I've also used a penlight, holding it with my teeth. Mouthing the light in this manner also focuses a small beam right where you need it. It can be a problem enunciating, however, if you suddenly need to warn your partner, "Heh! Wook out for that yock!"

As the evening deepens, fishing may become more somnolent, despite the frogs bellowing along the bank or the bats winging erratically. When the bites are few or far between, it's easy to close your eyes—and who would know? But a striking bass, like a water moccasin on the front porch, rouses you instantly. You slide up on the edge of your seat and squeeze the foregrip of your rod with conviction—primed to set the hook. Fingering the monofilament and holding the rod tip high, you feel something swat the line. You swing for the fences, only to find a bat—not a bass—has done you in.

Fluttering bats, squinting at knots, and more backlashes than you'd care to admit—what happened to the pleasures of fishing after-hours? You zip up your Windbreaker and stow your rods, still hoping to find your way back, when a silhouette emerges—a tree not far away. Other shapes appear; you glance first at your watch and then toward the east. The stars are fading. Another summer day is waiting in the wings and you look to your partner, "Hey. Hand me that tackle box. We've still got a few hours before breakfast."

53

The targets don't change as the light fades at evening time—only your perspective. Casting gets a little trickier, and a sense of touch must replace your reliance on sight. But not so with the bass. Within an hour its vision is well adjusted, and it begins a night of efficient predation.

Lake Chickamauga, Chattanooga, Tennessee (above), by Monte Burch. International Falcon Reservoir on the Rio Grande River, Texas (left), by Willard Clay.

Harris Chain Lake, Florida, by Jim Vincent.

Dollar on the first fish? Dollar on the
big fish? Pay up, gentlemen! So the winner gets a little giddy—even the losers
don't mind when a really big bass comes aboard.

Private phosphate pit near Dunnellon, Florida, by Lionel Atwill.

Some days are especially fulfilling, like those whose ceremonies end with brilliant amber lights in the west. Trying to stretch the moment, we make that final cast of the day—maybe a couple more. And then it's gone, and we yearn to do it again.

South Fork of the Shenandoah River, Virginia, by Lionel Atwill.

A bass boat is not always a status symbol, but it is an emblem of the independent nature of the bass fisherman as he pursues his quarry. The boat lets him get away—if only a few hundred yards.

59———

Grand Lake, Oklahoma, by Lionel Atwill.

That independence extends to anyone who is willing to step to the forward platform and begin the chase in earnest. For those with knowledge of bass behavior and a practiced casting hand, the bass is an equal opportunity game fish.

San Vicente Lake, California, by Lionel Atwill.

Not everyone leaves the dock with a fervent desire for taking bass, but on those reservoirs with big-fish reputations, the thought of hooking one is never too far from consciousness. Let a good one yank a bobber under in the fog or break a wimpy rod, and see who comes back with a change of heart.

Orange Lake, Florida, by Kitty Pearson-Vincent.

The serious bass fisherman is focused. He has a plan for each part of the day, and he tries to make use of every fleeting moment. Before the fog can burn away, he may "flip" his way along a flooded shoreline, his stout rod and heavy monofilament primed to eliminate break-offs.

The smallmouth never fails to impress a captor—or a would-be one. Winnipeg River System, Manitoba, by Wade Bourne.

ONLY THEIR MOUTHS ARE SMALL

I figured it must have been a crank call when the voice said, "Do you want to go river fishing for smallmouth?" Where I live the nearest riverbed is an hour's drive. The nearest one with water is over a hundred miles away. But the caller persisted. He had just come back from a trip to the *lower* Kern River, where he had encountered some surprising action. "Don't miss this," he urged. "I'm getting thirty fish a day just minutes from town."

It sounded good but I was dubious, and just as soon as I got off the phone, I pulled out a map of Southern California and tracked the blue line where it emerged from the western slope of the Sierra Nevada. The upper Kern, both the main fork and the south fork, has an excellent reputation for trout, including some native browns. The middle portion of the river, on the other hand, often receives stocks of rainbows and is a favorite run for whitewater rafting. But the Kern also has a more insidious reputation as a deadly flow that accounts for more annual fatalities than any other such waterway in the country. Still this was the lower Kern and a chance at smallmouths, so I decided to risk it.

We had determined to start the drift (some 4 miles of the river) about midmorning, allowing ample time and daylight to capture the setting on film. But while I had imagined the trip in some kind of sturdy riverboat, instead I found a wobbly johnboat strapped to the back of my host's pickup. The craft, painted olive green above the waterline but bare metal on the hull, may once have served ably as a duckboat. But looking at the warped gunwales and a pair of bailing buckets, I wondered if we weren't setting ourselves up to be a couple more Kern River casualties. Driving eastward out of town, we skirted the last bits of civilization, until we came to a turnout that accessed the river. There, like reluctant pallbearers, we slid the johnboat off the trailer and unceremoniously dragged the craft to the water's edge. Since no slack water was available, launching in the current was similar to parallel parking on ice. With the boat sliding down the bank, there was no choice, the last guy in got his feet wet. Still, the floor inside the boat was dry, and the thought of river smallmouths dancing on the end of my line was a sure cure for motion sickness.

Soon I let go with a cast toward a gravel bar, but the current slung my little jig downstream before it could sink. Although I was able to reel in and make several rapid-fire casts, the same thing continued to happen, and I began to wonder how anyone could catch anything at such a pace. Just when I was about to tie on a heavier lure, my guide for the day served up two piercing thoughts: "I've never been this far upriver before," and "It looks as if we're coming up on some rapids!" Sliding over to the center of the bench seat for balance, I

grabbed the gunwales and closed my eyes, hoping that I wouldn't get to town before my partner did.

Somewhere below the second stretch of whitewater (the polite term is "riffles") the river slowed and with it, my pulse. There, at the foot of an old railroad bridge, I caught my first river smallmouth. True to form, it jumped twice and streaked cross-current before I finally lifted it aboard and removed the hook from its tiny mouth. Although barely 8 inches long, it pulled like a much larger fish. I was impressed. Repeating the process frequently over the next several hours eventually erased my earlier misgivings. Yet I couldn't help but wonder how it must be to take a really hefty smallmouth.

Admittedly, the Kern is hardly a trophy fishery. In fact, the very best streams—those sporting fish ranging 12 to 17 inches or more—are all located over on the right side of the country, including the upper Mississippi above the Twin Cities, the Saint Lawrence in New York, and a whole series of rivers winding through Pennsylvania, Maryland, and Virginia. But the most prodigious smallmouths have actually come from reservoirs. Dale Hollow on the Cumberland River between Kentucky and Tennessee is the home of the world record fish. And nearly 70 percent of all state records have come from impoundments. Life for the smallmouth bass is somehow easier in deep, clear, still waters—wherever they are found.

The West touts a few such spots, some more familiar than others. Among the rugged cliffs of the Tonto National Forest and on the very edge of the Apache Trail in central Arizona, Apache Lake and its smallmouth treasure remain hidden from the greater bands of fishermen. Although Apache Lake is closer in miles to civilization than the larger and more popular Theodore Roosevelt Lake upstream, the harrowing climb above Apache Junction past Tortilla Flats and then up the unpaved lip of the canyon makes traffic control easy. Without guardrails or lights, the trail features two-way traffic—one way at a time. Getting to the lake quickly is not the issue, just getting there is.

Still, we made the climb—Phoenix resident Lou Starkey and me—bass boat in tow, waiting until after sunrise to tackle the switchbacks. We had chosen a weekday hoping to avoid any traffic that might be coming down the mountain. Cornering gingerly to keep the truck and trailer from sliding, we finally reached the crest and viewed the deep blue glaze that filled the canyon floor. It was then that I seriously considered taking up residence, if not for the beauty of the place, then certainly to avoid the trip back down.

That perspective had no reason to change once we picked up our third partner, pro fisherman Bob Lee, at the marina and then launched the boat. Although this was desert country, it was hardly the moonscape of the lower Kern. The sage was beginning to bloom, and on every ridge and mountainside the saguaro cactus saluted. Along the water's edge were classic smallmouth structures. Sheer rock cliffs, tapering deep into the clean water, formed the northern shore, and rockfalls and boulder points were numerous. On one of these rubbled banks, I got all I could bargain for.

Three of us were tossing small jigs and plastic worms when something nudged my smoke-colored worm but wouldn't commit. "I think I got tickled," I offered, casting to the spot again. Two casts later, the splitshot and trailing worm "got heavy"; I reeled through and set the hook. This bass may have been modest in picking up the bait, but the sting of the hook must have sounded general quarters below. The fish bolted out of the shallows and across the path of one of my partners, forcing me to scuttle to my left and dip the rod under his line. When I got to the transom, the fish dove directly under the boat and I backreeled furiously, hoping that it would stop.

It did, but unsatisfied with its position, it turned 180 degrees from the boat, aimed back toward the shore,

65

and then broke for the surface. General quarters had now sounded in our boat as well. My partners, both seasoned fishermen, knew I was into something. One grabbed for the net and the other pointed at the path of the line, barking the epithets of desperate men. On my knees, I tried to get the rod tip down, but it didn't matter. The fish came out of the water.

"What have I got on?!" I pleaded. The fish, backlit in the morning glare, was hard for me to see. "Is that a largemouth or what?"

"No way! That's a smallmouth," said netman Lee.

"That's a *big* smallmouth!" shouted Lou.

That the fish still wasn't done with me confirmed their assessment. Unable to free itself near the surface, the fish surged quickly toward the bow, pulling line off the reel and forcing the three of us to change positions on deck. The bass then cut back under the trolling motor and ran the length of the boat before breaking the surface once more when it reached the net. Twenty-one inches long and every bit of 5 pounds, it was a Sunbelt trophy. I've never taken such a ride in my life.

Later, there was some murmuring when I lowered the fish back over the side. "That's a wall fish out here, George." "That's sure a big one, buddy." And I was tempted, but something inside said not this time. After all, it was three against one, and the big bronze fish had battled us straight up. I'll come back again, that's a promise. And those bass better keep their big, er, small mouths closed when I do.

Saint Johns River, Welaka, Florida, by Lionel Atwill.

There are many parallels in the lives of bassin' men and their quarry. Often migrating through one part of the lake to another, the fish pause or even congregate in certain places called "breaks" or others called "holding areas." For the fisherman, such a place might be called "the Lodge."

Lake Hodges, California, by Lionel Atwill.

There's something in the upbeat pace of bass fishing that begins at a young age. Bicycles strewn, these boys scramble to make that first cast while the adults bustle on the dock, or nervously wait in line to launch their boats.

Lake Hodges, California, by Lionel Atwill.

W hen you're young, one of the best
things about breaks in the fishing is taking another look at the fish, and then
another and another. The evidence seems to support the fishing and vice versa.
We grownups of course don't require this assurance.

Susquehanna River, Pennsylvania, by Lionel Atwill.

Some fishing traditions begin with
boyhood friends sharing an adventure together. Few things in life bond as well
or provide as many fond memories.

Lake Mattamuskeet, North Carolina, by Lionel Atwill.

Getting started is easy. It only takes the company of someone who cares enough to want you there. The casting methods and other tricks will come with time. But the love—that's gotta be there from the start.

Saint Johns River, Welaka, Florida, by Lionel Atwill.

In town, a restaurant may need both
good service and good food to survive. Out at the lake, good food is a bonus—as long
as the place has a tankful of live bait for sale. It's all a matter of priorities.

Carrollton, Georgia, by Lionel Atwill.

In the world of artificial baits the
catchword is "new" or "hot." The bubble gum–colored plastic worm may be
the hottest bait to open the decade. A gaudy enticer, this buoyant worm is
used to slither over the tops of grass beds.

ON RAINBOW
RIVER ONLY

SPEED LIMIT 20 M.P.H.
OCT. 16 TO APR. 14
NO WAKE IDLE SPEED
ONLY APR. 15 TO OCT. 15
MARION COUNTY ORDINANCE 85-17

ANGLERs
RESORT
DUNNELLON FL.

Withlacoochee River, Dunnellon, Florida, by Lionel Atwill.

Even the inland waterways and hidden passages have their own brand of civilization. Posted speed limits seem to coincide with the busy tourist months, but prime early spring months for bass are open to rapid transit.

South Fork of the Shenandoah River, Virginia, by Lionel Atwill.

And the honor system still works.
Bass fishermen's stories may be subject to question, but this weathered sign
attests to something better—the camp owner's trust in his fellow anglers.

Doing battle with a flippin' stick, a technique pioneered in the 1970s. Pomme de Terre Lake, Missouri, by Monte Burch.

Catch 'Em, Let 'Em Go!

You can always spend it," Dad used to say. "The trick is holding onto it." So I wonder, how many times as a zealous consumer did I pause reluctantly, tap my wallet, and then think better of it? Dad knew I'd have to watch my limited resources, and over time, with restraint, my family's had most of the things we've really wanted. That same lesson has not been lost on the black bass as a resource. The popularity of this sport fish has outgrown the fish's ability to maintain itself, but that same popularity has stirred a change in attitude among anglers. Stringer clips and braggin' sticks laden with fish are long left to scrapbooks—memorabilia of a different era. Today we still collect photos, but more often than not the catch is posed only for a moment before it's released to battle again.

Of course, the process of that attitude adjustment has taken some time. Arkansas's Billy Murray, former tournament pro and founder of the National Bass Institute at Indiana State University, describes the transformation of the bass-fishing conservationist: "First, all a fisherman wants to do is catch *one* bass. Then, having caught that one, and likely others over time, he hopes to catch a limit of bass. How long it takes to get that limit varies, but one day he does, and after many other limits, he sets his goal on a lunker bass. He fishes even harder now and more often, hoping to get a trophy bass on the wall. And finally, having caught that trophy fish, he sets out to catch a limit of lunkers. Then, after getting a limit of big bass, it's then he decides it would be good if we all released our fish."

It's curious that there could be such a gap in our attitudes about black bass, but consider the clarity of hindsight. Just 20 years ago a big stringer seemed to be the goal of every red-blooded young man who sported a B.A.S.S. patch (as a member of the Bass Anglers Sportsmen Society) or wished he had one. Broomstick rods and heavy line were regulation gear for what they called bass busting. With such stout tackle, you wanted to set the hook so hard, you'd "cross their eyes"! There was no malice toward the fish. This was men's work, and a bassin' man was measured by the size of his catch. Sporting magazines touted "can't miss" waters while featuring pictures of huge fish kills. "Look what I caught" or "top this if you can" were themes that urged us on.

And why not? During the boom years of reservoir construction and exploding bass populations in the 1960s and 1970s, bass demonstrated their prolific sunfish nature. Biologists claimed, and perhaps rightly so at the time, that bass populations could not be depleted by hook and line. Why not catch all you want, there were more than enough for everyone. What biologists couldn't have anticipated, however, was that the num-

ber of bass fishermen would increase a hundredfold between the 1960s and 1970s. And that this hoard of anglers, partly spurred by the latest fish-catching methods spawned from bass tournaments, would become a fish-harvesting army. About 1973 I remember one old-timer complaining, "Sh—. I remember a couple of years back I'd go out and get my limit in the morning and come back in the afternoon and get me another limit. It sure ain't what it was."

In 1972 the burgeoning Bass Anglers Sportsmen Society first announced its "Don't kill your catch" policy for its tournament circuit. Special decals depicting a bass in the cross hairs of a gunsight were distributed, and all the readers of BASSMASTER *Magazine*, not just those fishing in competition, were urged to set their fish loose. Unfortunately, that message was not as well received as the latest advice on catching bass. Portable sonars exposed new parts of reservoirs to angling pressure and efficient new techniques such as the shallow-water flipping method, which used an extra-long, heavy-action rod, and 20- to 30-pound test line, just gave the fish fewer places to hide.

But things have changed, and Dad would be pleased. Bass fishermen and enlightened fishery management specialists have contributed to better fishing through catch-and-release policies, both voluntarily and through regulation. One of the most remarkable fisheries in the nation, Lake Fork, an hour east of Dallas, Texas, may sport the best black bass fishing in the country. Combining faster-growing Florida bass, a slot limit that forbids taking prime spawning bass between 14 and 21 inches, and satisfied fishermen who are just grateful for the high-quality fishing and who are willing to return many of their fish to the water, Fork is a monument to bass conservation in this decade.

But at 28,000 acres, Lake Fork has a lot more room for error than its California counterpart, Lake Castaic, a 2,200-acre pond just 50 minutes from Los Angeles. The most heavily trafficked reservoir in the state, and one that has produced Florida intergrades in excess of 21 pounds, Castaic delivers thousands of recycled bass each year because bass fishermen have recognized their role in maintaining good fishing. Finding a boat trailer there without a catch-and-release bumper sticker is like finding one without wheels.

And it makes so much sense. The black bass, especially the largemouth, are hardy characters that stretch your line, bend your rod, and then, with proper han-

dling, swim away to do it again. The black bass was made for catch-and-release fishing. Just look at the size of that mouth. What a great "handle" it is; just put your thumb in and pinch its lower jaw with your forefinger and you have a no-slip grip. You can't do that with a barracuda. The bass can be lifted, unhooked, photographed, even kissed, and then lowered back into the water without the slightest damage to its gills or its protective slime coating.

Now the spirit of catch-and-release fishing has spurred even greater efforts in bass conservation. In 1987 the largest habitat enhancement and research project in the world was undertaken at the Lake Mead National Recreation Area, a 229-mile-long reservoir on the Colorado River between Nevada and Arizona. Under the direction of the University of Nevada at Las Vegas, and with the assistance of the Department of Wildlife and the National Park Service, more than 1,000 volunteers in 300 boats poured 20,000 gallons of ammonium polysulfate into the waters of the Overton Arm of the lake. The liquid fertilizer was introduced at a rate of 1 gallon per acre to spur algae growth and bolster the first level in the food chain. Increased amounts of algae mean increased forage for the zooplankton that feed the

79

threadfin shad and panfish fry that, in turn, feed the black bass and other predators. The project, funded by some $250,000 raised through matching federal funds over three years, received national press coverage. On-going studies of the effort have revealed the feasibility of recharging nutrient-poor waterways to the betterment of fishing.

This monster undertaking, however, had its roots in the "Christmas tree" project funded nearly three years earlier by Lowrance Electronics and contributions from tournament fishermen. I covered that project for the now-defunct *U.S. BASS Magazine* and saw firsthand a new concern among fishermen for their sport. Some 7,000 trees were collected in an empty lot in Hender-son, Nevada. The Christmas trees were to be used in a comparative study on how various types of cover or hab-itat would protect bass fry and attract baitfish to support the adult bass. The trees would be anchored at various depths to compensate for water level changes, and they would be monitored and compared to other habitats made of bales of hay or weighted clusters of nylon strands.

Struggling for hours, 65 volunteers—bass club mem-bers, scuba divers, and striper fishermen—standing shoulder to shoulder loaded the trees (except those with

flocking or dangling tinsel) into huge dump trucks for delivery to the lake. The parade of dump trucks followed by the volunteers headed toward Callville Bay. My pickup brought up the rear, stopping to collect a way-ward tree that had escaped. Admittedly, I was surprised by the number of participants, but the whole city seemed to get involved. One building supply house do-nated tons of brick to anchor the brush piles, and the trucks themselves were loaned on a "fuel-only basis." That was significant since the $3,000 budget had to cover everything from special permits to feeding the crews for two days. And yet, there was no complaining in the ranks when we got to the Callville turnoff and found the junction covered with snow—an ironic setting in the Nevada desert.

I climbed a hill above the launch ramp to photo-graph the activity. From my vantage point, I got a view of industry and a hint of how the job was perceived by the Department of Wildlife. Instead of the three prom-ised barges, there were two. Instead of direction and sup-port, there were uniformed men standing aside with grim faces. And the materials we had to use were primitive.

Putting my camera down, I grabbed a piece of the six-gauge solid wire the department had furnished and tried to twist it around the base of some trees. Volunteers clutched branches and held on while others secured them as best they could. The sharp-edged wire cut hands and jackets and the dry branches scratched uncovered skin, but the volunteers persevered. The bundles were then dragged across the launch ramp to the barges where the bricks had already been loaded.

About noon things began to change. The huge piles of trees were beginning to disappear as the barges made trip after trip. Wildlife officers began to stir, even smile. Suddenly a third barge appeared in the harbor. Still, there were budgetary limits and time constraints. The job had to be completed by Sunday afternoon. It was hard to believe that the group could make their bare-bones budget stretch over two days. I listened while the project coordinator dickered over the price of 20 buckets of chicken that Saturday, and yet everyone got fed, even the additional 50 volunteers who showed up on Sunday. Pride in the group swelled and the work was contagious. When a sleek, wood-decked cruiser—one reserved for VIPs in the Department of Wildlife—appeared and then headed out of Callville Bay with a bundle of trees on the foredeck, the issue was clear. Fishermen could make a difference.

Catch and release is working, and it's focusing attention on other logical efforts to enhance and sustain bass fishing. Habitat improvements such as constructing brush piles, fertilizing lakes, or planting willow trees around shorelines to provide shallow-water sanctuaries for the fish contribute to the future of bass fishing. Yes, spending the resource has been too easy, but we're finally learning the trick. We're learning how to hold onto it for tomorrow. For all the tomorrows.

Florida Everglades, by Kitty Pearson-Vincent.

Fishn Frank Medved does what many of us only dream about. Leaving the real world behind, he carries all that matters in his van—fishing gear and lure-making tools—on his endless quest for bass. Selling homemade lures and guiding now and then, he prospers on $2,000 a year.

Florida Everglades, by Kitty Pearson-Vincent.

83——

Sometimes his equipment is not as willing as Frank is. But he gives the starter cord another yank, and soon he'll be piloting his vintage aluminum rig into the bassing wilderness.

Florida Everglades, by Jim Vincent.

Frank's training as an engineer has served his bass fishing well. Having logged over 600 designs in surface spoons, he has baits for every condition and, from the looks of them, they all work.

Florida Everglades, by Kitty Pearson-Vincent.

He is an explorer and a pioneer in
every sense. Cutting through the sawgrass of the Everglades, Frank fishes where
few others have ventured—and relies on lures of his own design.

Florida Everglades, by Jim Vincent.

Alert to the changing environment
and the nuances of nature, Frank has patrolled the memorable bass waters of Florida
and Ohio for more than 20 years.

Florida Everglades, by Kitty Pearson-Vincent.

Hic first creations were fashioned from the mudflaps of an 18-wheeler, but there is nothing arbitrary in their construction. "Old Moe," his only mounted trophy bass, would be one to attest to that.

The modern bass boat has it all. Grand Lake, Oklahoma, by Charles J. Farmer.

BASS TRANSIT: BREAKING THE CODE

Call it "bass transit," if you will, the precipitating boat ride of the 1990s. Think of freeway driving in a convertible without a windshield, in a projectile with no brakes, whose only contact with the water is a 12-square-inch pad. At 70 miles per hour, your hairline stretches back like a Klingon warrior; your eyes flush past your ears. An unbuttoned collar slaps your face like playing cards clipped to a bicycle wheel, and you squeeze the grab rail till it bleeds.

That is a bass boat. And nothing is more symbolic of the evolutionary progress of bass fishing than this sleek, high-powered machine. Fitted with electronic gear, varied propulsion modes, and accommodations for the fisherman and his live cargo,

the bass boat is the emblem of a sport taken to its technical extreme. Yet is it not fitting that bass fishing's superenthusiasts would demand such a craft?

Consider the following angler evaluation by David Myers, a several-time executive for Fenwick rods and former fly-fishing guide and manufacturer's representative for Forrest Wood's renowned Ranger bass boats: "The trout fisherman pursues the 'experience' first, which includes an appreciation for the whole environment, and he tries to place himself in that pleasing setting of clean water and clean air. A fly-fisherman enjoys the quality and the achievement of effective casting, and of fly tying, and he enjoys catching fish—but it is not essential.

"The saltwater angler just likes tugging on fish.

Out on the water with no land in sight, the setting is not important. His idea of a good time is 'getting bit.' He's into 'suicide' by the fish and if it takes chumming a million little fish to get the big fish to come to the boat, that's fine. His tackle is designed to put more pressure on the fish so he can get it into the boat fast, so he can go catch another one.

"But the high-tech bass fisherman is something else. His ultimate experience is 'breaking the code,' figuring out exactly what it will take to find and catch fish on a given day. He's really half hunter and half fisherman. If he's really figured it out, he's just as excited if he had to use eighth-ounce jig heads and two-inch purple grubs in twenty-five feet of water on the shady bluffs of the east side of the lake, as he would be to fish white spinnerbaits with gold willow blades in two feet of water around the eel grass on the downwind side of the lake. Any of these anglers would like a big fish, but for the bass guy, he needs to crack the code."

The developmental process of this unique type of angler and his specialized fishing boat began innocently enough. In the early years, the flat-bottomed johnboat was the traditional rig. With a shallow draft and powered by a small outboard, paddles, or push-poles, it served well in the many ponds, sluggish rivers, and

backwaters of the Southeast where black bass, especially largemouths, dwelt in plentiful supply. First built of wood and later aluminum, the johnboat was the predator in the cypress-filled swamps. Sliding the boat off the levee like a gator looking for a meal, the early anglers approached bass fishing at a more primitive, relaxed level.

In time, the most innovative development was added—the electric "trolling motor." Instead of remaining in the stern to push the boat, this motor pulled and maneuvered the first "bass boats" from the bow. Adding a new measure of control with this quiet stalking ability, the bass fisherman became more efficient and even more successful. Progress continued. Fore and aft pedestal chairs and live boxes or wells to carry the catch were added, but the narrow beam stayed. Eventually, designers incorporated a more stable, tri-hull configuration and finally added casting platforms or decks to raise the fisherman higher above the water for more effective casting. These were the boats first identified with bass tournaments.

As bass fishing and professional competition turned to the larger manmade impoundments, further changes occurred. In the mid-1970s, high-performance hulls borrowed from boat racing made their debut. My first encounter with them was in 1975. I was competing in my second-ever bass tournament in a 15-foot tri-hull with a 65-horsepower engine. These new boats with their helmeted drivers sped down the lake, leaving the rest of us trailing their rooster tails. "Boats with a hundred and fifteen horses are crazy," I mumbled. But those guys were already fishing by the time I reached the far end of the lake. And with a 2:00 weigh-in, they fished longer and still made it back on time.

A dozen years later, sporting 200 horses and riding the latest in high-performance double-step hull design, I again marveled at how the other competitors' boats passed me with equal disdain—just as in the old days! Many bass fishermen covet speed beyond any other feature of their boats, even beyond their ability to catch bass. While the Southeast and much of the country have adopted a 150-horsepower limit on bass boats, the West, with its big Colorado River reservoirs, finds speed the answer to increased fishing time through decreased running time. More than once I've lined up against 300-horsepower engines—and I haven't caught up yet.

There always seems to be a sense of urgency in the life of the high-tech bass angler. While his boat is hurtling through the water, his mind is racing as he tries to "break the code" and find the fish, or bring his catch to the weigh-in site. When you understand this about the

bass fisherman's nature, then the equipment used seems to make more sense.

Take the surface temperature meter. Since bass are a "warm-water species" (most active in 50–80°F water), this unit quickly identifies which parts of the waterway have the most suitable conditions for holding catchable bass. Then there's an even more sophisticated piece of equipment—the pH meter—for measuring the relative acid/alkaline levels of the water. Bass tend to thrive in a pH range of 7.0 to 9.0, even when living in water that has a low oxygen content. When the fishing action subsides, it usually means that the pH is unsuitable.

However, no piece of equipment has done more for broadening the horizons of the bass fisherman than the sonar, and no properly rigged bass boat would take to the water without at least one (if not two or three) on board. By rapidly firing sound waves toward the bottom and then retrieving the signals and interpreting them on a dial, pixel screen, or advancing graph paper, these units can determine bottom depth, bottom composition, and even water density. They can also discern various bass hideouts—such as weed beds, stumps, and rocks—or the presence of baitfish, and, of course, whether there are any larger fish, including bass, in the area.

So how does the otherwise prudent individual obtain the ultimate fishing machine, with its five-digit price tag? How, for instance, would the "other half" acquiesce to the not-so-hidden passions of his or her partner? In many cases, the fishing/racing package must be disguised as the "family boat." Rick Grover, owner of the top dealership in the nation for Champion bass boats, revealed the following about the bass boat purchase: "When a guy brings his wife in, we already know *he* wants the boat. We talk strictly to the wife. Dual consoles with windshields (giving the passenger and the driver equal protection from the wind and cold), bimini tops, and padded deck covers for lounging are the items that make the boats attractive and make the sale." And to give you a feel for how significant passenger comfort has become in the market, 85 percent of the boats Grover sells have the dual console interior.

Before you get the idea that bass boat dealerships are strictly the realm of slick-talking salespeople, consider that boat dealerships are also service centers that must endure the inevitable I-should-be-out-on-the-water-*now* attitude of most high-tech bass chasers. It's no wonder many bass boat dealers walk the fringes of sanity.

Bo Dowden, former bass-fishing world champion and busy Ranger boat dealer in Natchitoches, Louisiana, described a typical nightmarish encounter with one of these bass boat nuts: "Most problems stem from trying to make simple things hard. But what happens is some guy who just spent fifty or a hundred dollars to get his motor running picks up his boat, takes it out in a hurry, and it don't run. He comes back, huffin' and puffin' and he won't tell you anything more than 'It was runnin' when I brought it in here and now it won't even fire up!' Well, naturally, you want to make him happy and you start checkin' things. You put the motor in the test tank, and this guy is right over your shoulder and raisin' Holy Sam Hill. You test all the instruments, and by now he's got you so you're not thinkin' straight. 'What could we have done to this motor?' Then up on the screen it comes: *Disconnect black-and-yellow wire.* This guy forgot to connect his kill switch! The motor couldn't start if it wanted to. It's enough to give you gray hairs."

But that's the nature of the bass boater. Steeped in bass-fishing knowledge and immersed in technology, he's ever ready to "crack the code" and uncover the secrets of catching bass. Failing that, however, he has, on board, an expanded file of meteorological, biological, and even philosophical explanations to cover the most meager catch. And why not! After all, a bass boat has everything.

Lake Powell, Utah, by Charles J. Farmer.

93————

The bass fisherman's boat is just one
of the tools he may use to locate and catch fish. While their appearances may
vary, their function is the same—to take him to the most likely bass hideout.

Private pond, Front Royal, Virginia, by Lionel Atwill.

Pond for pond, the canoe can hold its
own against any other type of fishing craft. When a fisherman is ready for sonar,
or trolling motors, or gelcoat—he'll get it. But then, too, he may never switch.

Laurel, Mississippi, by Don Wirth.

Pad baits, like weedless Rats, have a curious
appeal all their own. While they may not fool a graduate student in biology,
the bass feel differently. When retrieved with an air of seeming helplessness, or
occasional frantic motion, they may be met with vicious acceptance.

Lake Elsinore, California, by George Kramer.

The sky is often a portent to the fishing.
A dry winter morning in the West is cool and blue and a settling high-pressure
zone usually means mild afternoons, but reluctant postfront bass. Of course, it
doesn't stop anyone from fishing.

Winnipeg River System, Manitoba, by Wade Bourne.

Muggy summer days as a warm front pushes through Canada's midwest are a different story. A noisy topwater bait like a Baby Zara Spook or perhaps a buzzbait will stir a response this morning and again later, just before dark.

Lake Mattamuskeet, North Carolina, by Lionel Atwill.

This Carolina boat provides everything
needed for good bass fishing. Its classic lines fit its quiet environment perfectly.

Stockton Lake, Missouri, by Charles J. Farmer.

Everybody has a recipe for bass, and every once in a while we like to try it out. No apologies needed—except for that tartar sauce on your chin.

Team tournament fishermen share the road to the ramp. Lake Hodges, California, by Lionel Atwill.

BIG BUCKS ON THE LINE

Twenty-two hours straight through to Dallas and another four to Sam Rayburn stick in my thoughts like watermarks left on the hull. Rayburn, a famed East Texas reservoir, was to be the site of my first national bass tournament, and I savor those moments more today than when they first whistled through the wind-wings of my partner's van. Pushing it to the limit, we crossed half the country through rain showers and February chill, hardly stopping for gas or food—or wanting to. No, there were hooks to sharpen, maps to study, plans to assemble, and a thousand questions I never asked. A bass tournament can do that to you.

What an amateur I must have been, failing to tap the resource in the seat beside me. Gary Klein, a transplanted Californian now living in Montgomery, Texas and one of the nation's best tournament bass anglers, was at the wheel. Though only 25 years old, he was already a national champion and certainly a figure to be reckoned with wherever he launched his rig. Klein's tournament experience, fishing savvy, and close relationship with an even bigger star in the game—Rick Clunn of Montgomery, Texas—made him one of the most recognizable figures on the tour. I had a living encyclopedia of bassing to myself, yet just the chance to sleep under the pines in that tackle-strewn van, buck the churning waves of "Big Sam," and fish with the storied names in the sport was enough for me.

The tournament, sponsored by the Bass Anglers

Sportsmen Society (B.A.S.S.), was a three-day affair with maybe $30,000 in cash and prizes for the winner. Before the actual competition started, three days of "practice" were held so that anglers could test the waters, trying to locate reliable concentrations of bass, and figure out which lures would attract the fish.

Klein and I set out to do just that on the opening round, embarking from Twin Dikes Marina at the south end of the lake. Catching the forward end of yet another early spring frontal system, we slowly moved diagonally across the wide basin of corrugated water. The winds were steady out of the north, but not with the gusto that would eventually come as the storm front passed. Since the breeze was mixed with heavy intermittent rainfall, the weather forecaster apparently felt no need to show the tourists everything at once.

It was a time to enjoy. As is often the case under such weather conditions, the bass were in excellent spirits, striking a variety of fast-moving lures. We caught fish that weighed up to 6 pounds over beds of hydrilla (an aquatic weed), and every "textbook" bush or tree seemed to hold a bass. The foul weather even subsided for a time, or else we didn't notice because we were too busy catching fish.

About 11:00, I thought there might have been a patch of blue overhead, when the hole filled and the pine-lined bay darkened. Low over the water a heavy mist moved in, and then the serious rain struck. Still working our way along the shore, we cast Rattletraps toward the buckbrush and willow-lined points, when lightning shattered the air above the treetops. How can I describe it? Was it like rocket or cannon fire 30 or 40 feet over our heads? It was no less fearful. And it kept up. The rain pounded even harder. For 10 minutes, which seemed far longer, it swallowed us until I could no longer see my partner's face just 10 feet away. In our near-helpless state, all we could do was marvel—and laugh. Gary beached the boat to wait out the storm. Feeling the rain leak through my thin rainsuit and watching the boat fill up with water, I wondered, "Is this what tournament bass fishing is all about?"

The answer, of course, is yes. In the midst of the electrical storm, we laid down our highly conductive graphite rods. After all, this was only practice. But had the tournament been underway, it would have been hard to quit while the fish were biting. Maintaining a 5- or 6-cast-per-minute pace is the key to beating the clock in competition—the more casts, the more chances to catch fish. But that pace takes it out of you. You're standing—always standing—barely pausing to eat and trying to keep your balance on a moving deck. The intensity of the game grips the muscles in your neck and shoulders. When you finally step out of that boat, all you want to do is rest.

So each night during the practice period, Klein and Clunn, with me in tow, retreated to the campground, away from the hub of activity at the host resort and marina. Clunn wanted to isolate himself from the conversation and rumors associated with the fishing crowd. When he was strategizing and analyzing weather and water conditions, he didn't want to hear that "so-and-so was getting 'em on chartreuse crankbaits" or that "the big fish are in the willows." Empirical by nature, Clunn relied on his own observations or perhaps on information that he could obtain from a reliable source like his running mate, Gary Klein. It annoyed Clunn that so many fishermen seemed to take the contest lightly.

Small groups of anglers moved from campsite to campsite making small talk, and when they found Clunn's rig, they always stopped. Some of the faces I recognized from covering the tournaments for a bass-fishing publication; others were strangers. But merely keeping company with two giants in the sport somehow elevated me in the eyes of these boisterous visitors. I remember one particular round of introductions when Klein

pointed to me and said, "This is George Kramer from out in California." I was stunned when one of the guys responded, "Yeah, I think I've heard of you." And he wasn't even a relative!

On the evening of the final wind-wracked day of practice, the entire field of 250-odd contestants met in the crowded hall where the next day's pairings were announced. From the start of professional tournaments in 1967, random pairing of each day's partners by drawing has been used to prevent collusion. After all, before a contestant could cheat the field, he would have to cheat the other person riding in his boat, and none of the fiercely independent, highly competitive pros would ever stand for that. Each pair of anglers then met briefly, determining generally where they would be fishing and what types of tackle they would be using. Since I had entered the tournament without a boat, I was paired with an angler who had brought one. But several other pairings matched two boat owners, and those discussions were often spirited as one tried to convince the other to "come with me." More often than not, such "discussions" were terminated with the flip of a coin— unsatisfactory, but final. And the scene would repeat itself on the eve of each competition day.

In the end, this six-day venture became a crash

course in professional bass fishing. A crash course, indeed. The elements, especially the rain, I discovered, are the constant companions of the bass fishing tour— in New York or Florida or Texas—it doesn't seem to matter. But the wind is the worst, and the wind shattered my dreams at Rayburn. I had counted on those three practice days to familiarize myself with the lake, but following the wet first round, north winds turned the lake into a frothing sea, too dangerous to ford. Unprepared, unfamiliar, and unseasoned, I became yet another victim of the tournament game, weighing just 5 pounds of bass over three days. In a game of supposed ounces, winner Denny Brauer of Missouri barely nipped me by 50 pounds.

For all my previous fishing experience, I still had entered uncharted waters. The professional-level tournament (like this one at Sam Rayburn), or the more relaxed team or buddy tournament, differs from recreational fishing in more ways than just the payoff. Every morning each contestant's boat is inspected for the presence of live baits—only artificial lures are permitted— or live fish in the wells and for the required safety equipment. Furthermore, all boats are required to leave from and return to the same location at prescribed times. Rarely does a tournament fishing day last longer than

nine hours, but for every minute a boat is late to its appointed weigh-in, a pound is deducted from the competitors' totals.

Today's bass boats are equipped with aerated live wells so that each contestant can keep his catch alive for release after weighing, but tournament limits are restrictive and all bass must be a minimum length (12, 13, or even 16 inches). Likewise, bag limits (the number of fish each angler may have in possession) are usually less than those enjoyed by the public. In the pro tournament, each angler is scored individually and the one with the heaviest cumulative weight is declared the winner. However, in a buddy tournament, the weights of both anglers' catches are combined.

Touted as a tournament, another type of fish-for-money event—the big fish "derby"—has been on the scene for decades. Although offering substantial cash prizes, these contests are loosely structured and difficult to police. After paying their entry fees, anglers are often free to fish a lake for several days and nights without restrictions on bait or method. Entrants then bring their catch to a common site for weighing. Derbies appeal to a wide range of anglers including kids and other recreationalists because of the lack of restrictions, but they also open the door for fraud. One of the most publicized cases saw a pair of Texas brothers almost win a $50,000 prize with huge bass they had imported from Florida!

Such instances put a black mark on a sport that has grown steadily since the early 1970s. One-hundred-dollar entry fees and $1,000 prizes have grown to $600 entry fees and $30,000 top prizes on "tour" events. On the fishing tour, the pros accumulate points (or pounds), in addition to their money earnings, and the highest point totals send the top fishermen to a year-end championship. On the line in competitions such as the BASSMASTERS Classic, though, is more than the $50,000 in prize money. Due to the media attention and sponsor interest, a Classic winner could cement several years of income through endorsements and significantly raise his stature among his peers and the angling public.

In 1981 the first professional-style tournament ever to offer a $50,000 cash prize was staged at Lake Mead, and 155 anglers laid down $1,250 each for the opportunity. That event became the U.S. Open the following year, and for seven consecutive summers in the Nevada heat, the top bass pros in the country competed. Rick Clunn won twice, in 1984 and 1986, and Gary Klein took the top prize in 1988. Outside the BASSMASTER's main event, the U.S. Open became the most prestigious and influential bass tournament in the coun-try. A young Californian, Rich Tauber of Woodland Hills, actually launched his entire fishing and promotional career worth several hundred thousand dollars with a win in 1982. Although he has rarely visited the winner's circle since then, Tauber's 0.35-pound margin of victory demonstrated the financial impact of land-ing—or losing—a single bass in competition. Those fractions of a pound cost the runner-up at least $30,000.

After covering the Open as a member of the media for six years, I replaced my notepad and camera with 1,250 bucks. Entering the 1987 event, which produced the toughest fishing and lowest winning weight in the history of the tournament, I managed to catch just seven small bass in the four days of competition. Yet those 12 pounds of fish put me in 40th place among 266 of the nation's best.

Ironically, that skimpy catch was 20 places better than Denny Brauer, the man who'd thrashed me in my first national tournament. With that once-in-a-lifetime success, as much as the paycheck, I got a taste of what motivates the pros. It's a desire—more a compulsion—to measure up to your fishing peers. It's a test to find and catch bass under every condition—to do it when there's money on the line and while the clock is ticking.

The weigh-in's at 3:00. I'll look for you.

Grand Lake, Oklahoma, by Lionel Atwill.

Chris and Burma are on good fish, I just
know it. I wonder if Cathy is running to Honey Creek? And what's this weather going to do?
I hope I don't need that other flippin' stick in the van. Hmph. Let's get this thing started."

107

Grand Lake, Oklahoma, by Lionel Atwill.

Thank you.
Thank you. Thank you!"

Dale Hollow, Tennessee, by Don Wirth.

Three's company during the practice
rounds of a tournament, and maybe the winterlike chill will send them in early.
There'll be no such luxury once the anglers are paired off and the
competition starts.

Lake Griffin, Florida, by Jim Vincent.

109

Y ou hate to see 'em jump in a
tournament. All that head-shaking and summersaulting is great for the TV
audience, but it's nothing but Ulcer City when there's money on the line.
Murphy must have been a bass pro—"If something can go wrong, it will."

Lochloosa Lake, Florida, by Kitty Pearson-Vincent.

R*eaction bait fishing* is a term borrowed from the professionals. A "prop bait" with blades churning is sputtered across the surface hoping to draw a reaction from an otherwise inactive bass. It works. Sometimes.

Rainbow River, Florida, by Jim Vincent.

How many times do bass see a lure and not react? Underwater observers report that it occurs a lot more frequently than anyone might have guessed. Not only do the bass see the baits, they often follow them along before losing interest.

Arizona's Verde River in midsummer, a smallmouth haven, by Willard Clay.

DON'T BUG ME ABOUT FLY-FISHING

I t was against my better judgment that I ever took up bass fishing in the first place, and it was particularly unreasonable that I would try it with a fly rod. I've spent more than 20 years practicing conventional bass tactics, and faithfully heeding tournament rules that specifically prohibit fly-fishing. Was there any practical reason to switch? I had to be convinced. I was told that besides being steeped in tradition, fly-rodding is a growing sport. Not only that, avid fly-fishermen specifically mention *bass* as their next most popular quarry—when they're not pursuing trout in some postcard setting. To become a complete bass fisherman, then, it was vital that I become acquainted with this timeless fishing method.

Succumbing to such logic, I took up the long rod, not quite sure what was in store. After all, it had been my experience that fly-fishing was especially suited to certain elitist anglers who held their salmonid noses a bit too high for my tastes. When I first asked a flytier from a prominent shop about keel-hooked Wooly Worms for bass, he sneered, pooh-poohing the idea and referring to black bass as "those stupid fish." Since I've spent my entire fishing career in the understanding and pursuit of bass, you can imagine how pleased I was to deal with such an engaging personality. If bass were such fishermen's *second choice*, could it be they had made the selection alphabetically? And if so, how unfortunate that they had passed over *alligators* or *anacondas*.

But patience is something that bass fishing has taught me, and I attempted to bury those memories by reading all that I could about fly-rodding for bass. Bass bugs, in particular, held my interest. These floating chunks of cork or tightly wrapped deer hair and other materials were akin to the many surface plugs I'd often slung with baitcasting or spinning gear. Catching bass "on top" with bulky, visible lures surely showed that flyrodders couldn't be all bad.

Being new to it all and figuring I probably wouldn't recognize a Light Cahill from a heavy one, I sought out someone close to home to train me in proper fly-casting techniques. Jim Brown, the lakes program manager for San Diego's renowned trophy bass lakes, accepted the challenge of teaching an avowed "bass buster" but he offered an admonition, "When I teach someone, I don't let them bring any other kind of tackle into the boat."

That made sense to me. Learning any new technique requires commitment. It didn't matter that my first lesson would be held on a body of water not yet open to the public. Or that this little lake was marked with flooded timber, brush, and reeds or that it was reputed to be teeming with bass.

On the morning we set out for Barrett Lake, Jim appeared excited, despite his ready access to all the city's waterways. He talked of his successful adventures there in his younger days, and how, more recently, he and Fish and Game biologists had used an electroshock method to gather thousands of bass for a study of the lake. He had to be feeling good. We were on the verge of the most successful fly-fishing lesson he had ever given.

Passing through a series of locked gates and traveling along a narrow dirt road, we reached a mesa overlooking the boat dock. There we quickly loaded a wooden boat with cameras and several rods and pushed off into open water. Jim pointed to one of his 8½-foot rods that was lying in two sections and said, "Use that one."

Once I finally got the 7-foot leader and several feet of floating line pulled through the tip, I began to understand the difficulty in casting a bass bug. Dressed in rubber-band legs and feathers, the thing had all the mass of a cotton swab. I used to think casting a Rapala was tough, but that balsawood minnow casts like a ball bearing compared to the bug. Indeed, you don't cast the *lure* at all. It is the swinging of the thick, tapered line that actually delivers the lure. In truth, only arm wrestling is as awkward. Your elbow, not your wrist, imparts the actual motion of the rod. And there is no follow-through, just a robotic repetition of raising the rod to the vertical or 12 o'clock position and, after a momentary pause, tomahawking it to about 10 o'clock. In theory, the leader and bug will follow the forward end or shooting head of the line as you lower your rod tip.

After about 15 minutes of this, Jim was convinced that I wasn't going to get any better, and we headed for the far shore where flooded growth lined a steep embankment. It was inviting water and, considering the precipitous terrain, it was unlikely that even the most desperate poacher could have beaten us to the spot. Paralleling the bank, Jim began delivering a series of textbook casts, tucking the bug tight to the shoreline. I had to pause in admiration—and anticipation—for such lure placement surely meant a fish would strike. Stripping line, he made the bug come alive, and yet there was no response. When the bass didn't show, even on the choicest stretch, he finally revealed that I could "break my wrist" in order to lay the bug on the water. My accuracy improved, but the fish count didn't.

A couple of hours later, still fishless and with my elbow throbbing, it was time for radical measures. "OK," I thought, "I've learned to cast. Now it's time to catch some fish." Pulling a stowaway baitcaster from beneath the fly rods, I dug a willowleaf spinnerbait from my camera bag—kept there for emergencies, of course—and tied it to the 20-pound test. Perhaps deflated by our lack

of success with the bugs, Jim tied on a weighted streamer and shrugged, "Go ahead and throw it."

When we emerged from a wooded cove a couple of hours later, my "hardware" had accounted for 25 bass. The streamer, maybe half a dozen. "You could have had my house, my car, if you'd bet me we wouldn't catch a bass on a popper," my mentor confessed. But I was gracious. After all, I'd learned the basics of fly casting and had caught a nice bunch of bass to salvage the day. And heck, what would a real bass fisherman do with another BMW or a condo in La Jolla?

Still fishing popping bugs for largemouth is only part of the fly-rodding experience. The test would be to match wits with the wily smallmouth bass and to do so in the fabled rivers of the East—like the Potomac, the Susquehanna, and especially, the Shenandoah. This undertaking, however, would require additional outfitting, so I ordered the best equipment I could find and then waited for UPS to deliver.

Meanwhile, a more dreaded task was at hand. I still needed to visit a fly shop and purchase those items I couldn't find anywhere else. Alone and fearful of another snubbing, I waited in the parking lot, reading over an article on nymph fishing, until the shop was about to close. "OK," I rehearsed, "I have a seven-weight rod, I'll need seven-weight line. I'll be fishing bugs and nymphs. And I'll need tapered leaders, and some poppers . . . and yeah, some muddler minnows."

Mustering all my courage, I took a deep breath and swung open the door. "This looks like a place where real fly-fishermen hang out!" I don't know if that introduction worked, but I was in. Much to my chagrin, the place had "Madison River" written all over it. The carpet (a fishing store with a carpet?) was meet for the presidential suite, and the walls were lined with glass cabinets and neat little drawers like a doctor's office. A cluster of $300 fly rods glowered like an opera crowd.

Still, a jovial voice broke through, "What can I do for you?"

Again, I rehearsed my needs, but I couldn't keep a straight face. "Actually, I don't know too much about fly-fishing, but I'm heading back to Virginia to fish the Shenandoah."

"Well, you *sound* as if you know what you want. Let me show you some things."

I've never seen $75 spent so quickly or so painlessly. I bought 30 yards of floating line for $35—Lee and Joan Wulfe's best triangle taper. "Whew," I thought. "Mail-order I can buy 4,000 yards of monofilament for that much, put new line on every reel every trip, and still have some left at the end of the year! But I got the good stuff, and as much as I use a fly rod, I'll still have it when they bring back braided horsehair." I also bought a pair of 9-foot leaders for the price of another 400 yards of line, and by the time I had picked out a few bugs and a box to carry them in, three of my kids were going to miss Christmas.

On the eve of my flight, my new fly rod and reel arrived, and I discovered something else I didn't know. Those 30 yards of fly line would need 100 yards of backing to fill the spool. Not only that, I wasn't smart enough to figure out that I could spool on the fly line and then add the backing in order to get exactly the right amount. Had I done so, I could have unwound it and respooled it with the backing underneath. Using the "eyeball" method of estimating, I only needed four tries to get the spool filled. I almost missed my plane.

After a week of chasing largemouths on the tidal end of the James River in Virginia, I drove northwest from Richmond, finally arriving in the tiny town of Edinburg near the famed Seven Bends of the Shenandoah. But I wouldn't fish until I stopped to meet a fly-fishing legend—Harry Murray. We'd never met, but I'd called him several weeks earlier, hoping that we might chat or that he might direct me to a bit of productive smallmouth water. He did both, but in an unexpected environment.

The sign said "Fly Shop" all right, but right next to it was another sign saying "Pharmacy." Harry Murray, you see, is the local pharmacist as well as a bass-fishing guru. Indeed, as I entered the shop, I had to pass rows of patent medicines and foot-care products before I found a nook in the back where rods, reels, and a variety of flies and terminal gear were set in metal racks. Signage was handwritten and forthright—"Murray's Hellgrammite Assortment," "Whitlocks Hair Bass Bugs." And the prices were reasonable.

Tall and genteel, Murray broke away from his station behind the pharmacy counter to greet me, and for hours between phone calls for mail-order tackle and advice—or prescriptions and advice—I watched and listened. No customer's need was too small, no angler's request too troublesome. At a counter that made up a small coffeeshop–fountain, which he also ran, I chatted with his kids and his counter help. If ever there was a menagerie of entrepreneurial pursuits, it is Murray's Fly Shop. And when I walked out, I had more than a map and directions to the river. And more than a bag of Murray's Helgrammites.

Of course, it would take a lot more than that for me to catch anything with a fly rod. I parked close to the river near a deep riffle and tied on a muddler. Only a few yards away, a smallmouth cleared the water, and then, midstream, another showed itself. I entered the water and the current grabbed my jeans. I lurched slightly and tried to catch myself. My jogging shoes touched down on an algae-coated rock, and I slipped again. Clinging to my Browning Waterton, I wondered who might be watching as I struggled to stay upright.

Finally, somewhat stabilized, I placed the dull brown streamer a couple of rod lengths in front of me. But when it landed, I was puzzled. Wasn't the muddler supposed to be a sinking fly? Yet before this one could absorb water and before I could gather my thoughts, a 14-inch smallmouth darted out of nowhere and attacked the fly as it bobbed at my feet. I set the hook, but I didn't strip line at the same time and the fish was gone. Five minutes into my first streamside venture, I'd blown my chance, and it turned out to be my last one. Somewhere between Edinburg and the Maryland border, it must have been thundering. As I stood there numb, the flow suddenly surged, stirring up the water and pulling more like a riptide. I leaned against it, and then thought better of the idea.

No use drowning with a fly rod in my hand.

Brazos Bend State Park, Texas, by Willard Clay.

One of the myths about bass and
their habitat is that they variously remove themselves from an area as a matter
of seasonal migration. But, in fact, the bass in a given creek or bay are really
homers and just use different portions of the same area.

Oklawaha River, Florida, by Lionel Atwill.

119——

Comfort, protection, insulation from
heat or cold, a nursery for the kids, and a pleasant place to dine—it's home.

Lake Elsinore, California, by George Kramer.

I t's a touching story, of course, but flooded timber is more than prime bass habitat. While the fish may use the trunks and branches for protection, they are also highly touch-sensitive, actually needing bodily contact with the cover for their well-being.

Center Hill Reservoir, Tennessee, by Don Wirth.

121

Afundamental principle of bass behavior is not lost in the massive shadow of a highway bridge. A shaded location is often favored by bass, providing them a vantage point where their prey is always backlit. Still, the pilings would be more suitable targets for actual casting.

San Vicente Lake, California, by Lionel Atwill.

This armada is well attended, and a uniformed ranger admirals the last bucket of water from the flat-bottomed crafts. The routine is repeated daily—a part of the San Diego City Lakes tradition.

San Vicente Lake, California, by Lionel Atwill.

123

Some remembrances are especially striking
—like the shapes and colors of this City Lakes rental fleet. Anchors poised, the boats
are waiting to carry the day's bass-fishing hopefuls.

Many a tale was born in the swamps. Horseshoe Lake Recreation Area, Illinois, by Willard Clay.

COMPENDIUM OF BASS FISHING

And Other Lore

BASS & BASSIN'

There are a few things you can't enjoy in every state in the Union but, outside of Alaska, bass fishing isn't one of them. That availability, no doubt, may be the biggest reason that freshwater bass has become the most popular game fish in America. From coast to coast, in rivers, bayous, pits, and ponds, the bass is king and its followers are many.

The bass is also a fish with tradition. It was on this continent that some early British visitors to the Florida shore got a fishing lesson in the land of the Seminoles. Largemouth bass originally reigned in the more sluggish river systems of the East and Southeast, while their smallmouthed cousins dominated the cooler, though just as expansive, regions from the Great Lakes to what is now Tennessee. Some of the *Micropterus* genus have established their own niches in narrow ranges, whereas other species, like the Alabama spotted bass, have found new homes from Georgia to California. Black bass have endured generations of fish and fishermen, dams and pollution, transplantings and heavy harvests, bringing their own brand of selective pugnacity into the lives of hopeful fishermen.

Throughout their long residency in North America, fishermen have made ample and unusual attempts at catching bass, even though they may not always have known what they had. For instance, the term *green trout*, a misnomer for the largemouth, originated in 1773 and persisted well into the 1950s. But history, even fishing history, must have some parameters. Sports writers often refer to the "modern era" when speaking about records and performances, and students of bass fishing might do the same.

Certainly, the 1920s might be one place to hasten in the new era—a time when baitcasting reels were commonplace and wood was the primary material in lure manufacture. Who can deny the flavorful story of the Heddon Zara Spook? Produced in Michigan and first introduced in 1922, the cigar-shaped topwater bait was originally devised in Florida, where local fishermen compared its tail-walking motion to Pensacola's "girls on Zaragossa Street." Over time, the name was shortened to Zara and *spook* was added by the manufacturer to describe the skeletonlike rib pattern painted on the lure's sides.

Another more curious bass bait was developed during the same era. In Wisconsin in 1920 Alan P. Jones, founder of the Uncle Josh Bait Company, carved an imitation frog from a chunk of pork back fat because there was a shortage of the real thing that summer. The bait worked so well that Jones used his meat-processing company to supply the needed pig parts; he began selling the baits commercially in 1922. Having withstood the competition introduced by plastics, these pork-rind baits still catch bass as they did on Wisconsin's Jordan Lake so many years ago.

Other items have also had an impact on bass fishing. Since the introduction of the plastic worm, most notably by Nick Creme of Creme Lures, following World War II, there have been untold bass taken on these bogus crawlers, grubs, and eels. The very first ones were straight nightcrawler casts in nightcrawler colors, but since then salted, scented, and chemo-accented curl tails, ribs, pockets, and membranes have been added in limitless colors.

The arrival of graphite rods during the mid-1970s caused repercussions in bass fishing. On the one hand, no rods had ever been as light or as sensitive, and yet, many retailers were heard to mutter, "Who's going to buy a fifty-dollar fishing rod? Who's going to buy half a dozen?" Of course, the answer was not everyone. But hundreds of thousands of fishermen do. In the last 20 years, not only has there been a demand for better tackle, but also better and faster boats, stronger and thinner fishing line, and more sensitive and functional sonar. And the quest goes on.

While the chase is as intense as ever, there has been a change of heart regarding the bass. Although still revered, the bass is no longer quite the same object of machismo, where a stringer of fish was a statement of virility. The bass tournament still crowns a winner, record fish are still recorded, and the weekender lands all that he can. But often as not, the fish are offered a reprieve to battle again. We honor them:

Due to transplanting, the largemouth bass is found in every state in the continental United States, but it grows larger in a temperate environment. The "northern strain," *Micropterus salmoides salmoides*, grows to some

26 inches in length and about 15 pounds at maximum size, however, it probably averages less than 2 pounds nationwide. The Florida strain, *M. salmoides floridanus*, however, like the world record of 22 pounds 4 ounces, grows as large as 30 inches and would likely attain a weight of 24 pounds or more, given the opportunity. It eats virtually anything live that it can catch—fish, amphibians, reptiles, rodents, or birds—in its attempt to reach that size.

The smallmouth bass, *M. dolomieui*, is found in every state except Florida and Alaska, but it is well established from the Great Lakes to the Saint Lawrence River and through the upper Mississippi, Ohio, and Tennessee river systems and in many deep, clear lakes and reservoirs from New Hampshire to California. The world record of 11 pounds 15 ounces came from Dale Hollow Reservoir in Tennessee, but in most parts of the country, a 5-pounder would be a trophy. Its smaller maw (mouth closed, its jaw does not extend past the eye) gives the fish its name. Without a distinct black lateral line down the side, the smallmouth's bronze or copper coloring has led to the nickname "brownie" or "brown fish." The smallmouth also has a broad diet, but crayfish may top the bill, followed by leeches, minnows, and aquatic insects, depending on the locale.

The spotted bass, *M. punctulatus*, is most common in the waters of Kentucky, northern Alabama, Georgia, and Missouri, however, the world record of 9 pounds 4 ounces was established in California's Lake Perris. Sometimes referred to as a "Kentucky," the spotted bass is often found in rocky or cliff-bound areas. It is fond of crawfish and will also take all manner of

Another good fisherman on the water is a sign you're in the right spot. Orange Lake, Florida, by Kitty Pearson-Vincent.

minnows, shad, and fry. Although the average spot is usually under 2 pounds, it may be the most dogged of the black bass when hooked. Broken splotches of blue green above and below the lateral line give the fish its name, but its most identifiable characteristic is a patch of bristly teeth on its "tongue."

The shoal bass, *M. —*, is a genus without a species due to taxonomic questions over its similarity to the redeye bass. Fish identified as shoal bass have been recorded up to 8 pounds 3 ounces in Georgia, while the Alabama and Florida records are almost as large. The fish favors a fast-moving current and is found only in the limited range of three river systems—the Apalachicola in Florida, the Chattahoochee in Alabama, and the Flint in Georgia. The fish eats mostly crayfish. A colorful fish, the shoal bass sports a bronze-tinted back with greenish bands down the sides; its fins are usually a brownish red. Unlike the redeye, however, this larger fish features a prominent spot before its caudal or tail fin and another on the edge of its gill plate.

The redeye, *M. coosae*, is another fast-water black bass that prefers cool waters. It is much smaller than the shoal bass, rarely exceeding 1 pound. Its range is also limited to a few small streams in northern Alabama and to parts of Georgia and Tennessee. Bronze-backed with reddish fins, the redeye has distinct opaque white-and-bronze markings on the caudal fin. This tiny bass graduates to a crayfish diet after growing up on terrestrial and aquatic insects.

The Suwannee bass, *M. notius*, is another of the little bass with a limited range. Favoring shoal areas in the current, it exists in the drainage of the Suwannee and Ochlockonee rivers in northern Florida and, to a small degree, in southern Georgia. The world record, taken in Florida, is 3 pounds 14 ounces, measuring under 17 inches. The thick-bodied Suwannee almost appears to be a cross between a smallmouth and a spot. It favors crayfish over any other foodstuff.

The Guadalupe bass, *M. treculi*, is a Texas native found in the headwaters of the San Antonio River, the Guadalupe River, and parts of the Brazos and upper Colorado rivers. No larger than 4 pounds and looking much like a spotted bass, this small fish is at home in shallow running waters below riffles, although it has been successful in a few reservoirs where it had existed before impounding. In rivers, the Guadalupe feeds primarily on aquatic insects, however, it will adapt to other forage when living in reservoirs such as Lake Buchanan or Lake Travis.

FAST & FURIOUS

Upbeat and upscale are probably the two best ways to describe tournament bass fishing. Mobile and usually self-contained, the touring professional travels the country, logging miles like the highway patrol over land and on water.

Consider a typical tournament angler's trip log: Saturday, February 14, arrive Toledo Bend, Texas. Practice 15–17; tournament runs 18–20. Leave Saturday, February 21 for Florida. Stop 22–23, Atchafalaya Basin, Louisiana. Practice for April tournament. Drive the 24th (Tuesday) to Alabama; fish Guntersville 25–27. Stay for benefit tourney on Saturday the 28th. Leave Guntersville in the afternoon for Chickamauga in Tennessee. Fish Sunday and half of Monday, March 2, as prepractice for May tournament. Head for Sidney Lanier outside Atlanta; arrive Tuesday night. Fish Lanier March 4–5 (Wednesday and Thursday). Leave for Okeechobee in Florida, Friday morning. Arrive Saturday midmorning for rest (March 7). Practice period, March 8–10. Tournament, March 11–13 . . .

Not only is the pro on the run trying to make the best use of his travel time, but he has to have fishing licenses for a half-dozen states. No other type of fishing requires such a hectic pace or molds a fisherman's being. You can get a feel for it just by listening; the jargon, no matter

On the move, polyflake and chrome—high profile, high ticket, and high tech. Priest Reservoir, Tennessee, by Don Wirth.

what the dialect, reflects the kinetic essence of the sport.

Consider some of the lures they fish—"crankbaits" or "buzzbaits." A crankbait is retrieved by cranking the reel handle, usually at a fast clip. The buzzbait got the tag for its whirling, splashing topwater display. These are just two of several high-speed lures that the pros call "reaction baits." Unable to wait for those moments when the fish are actively feeding, the pro angler tries to incite a reaction from the bass with a lure that moves quickly or erratically. It's always go, go, go, trying to trim minutes between "honey holes." And even these prime fishing locations have been renamed. On the tournament milk run, they're merely called "stops."

"I rolled into my first stop and got two four-pounders on a buzzbait."

Because tournament bass fishing involves such a variety of water conditions coast to coast, the competitive crowd has also developed some colorful terms for regional types of fishing. Traditional down-home Southern bass fishing with big baits and heavy rods is contrasted with the subtle, ultralight equipment often required in the clear waters of the West. Heavyweight lures are referred to as "Bubba baits" or "power baits," while the petite, light-line Western bass lures are branded as "sissy baits." Since tournament bass fishing is a game in which the heaviest total weight wins, the trick is learning how to bring in the "big heads," that is, the bigger-size bass in the reservoir.

"If you fish them sissy baits, you ain't gonna get the big heads."

Despite the catch-and-release ethic prac-

ticed in all bass tournaments, competition has produced some curious idioms—in the possessive form—among the pros. Every contestant is required to turn in his daily catch for live release. You'll often hear the pro angler refer to an area where he has located bass as "my fish." And even more curious is the name given a fish that meets the minimum length standard of the contest; it's called a "keeper." Of course, these mobile bassers also carry appropriately transient excuses when they don't bring any keepers to the weigh scale. For example, one excuse that

Tournament anglers vie in a tag team match with a big Florida bass. Saint Johns River, Florida, by Jim Vincent.

you'll hear frequently is "my fish moved."

And yet, there is something in the chase that makes tournament bass fishing inviting. In addition to the thrill of speed and the accomplishment of the catch, the tournament fisherman like the race car driver is so identifiable. With his sleek, gel-coated vessel in tow, pedestals fore and aft, handrails and chrome wheels glistening in the sun, the bass pro is a high-profile kind of guy.

There are a lot of would-be professionals who covet the notoriety and lifestyle of the touring pro, and they are great imitators, often modeling their own rigs after those of the tour regulars. But with the fishing competition so intense, some anglers, looking for other ways to share the spotlight, attempt to grab an edge in the area of boat performance. One guy will have done a little engine work, added a jackplate to raise the motor and perhaps a special prop, and you'll hear him crow:

"Why, I blew off Roland Martin halfway up the narrows yesterday!"

That's just before he mentions his fish moved.

129

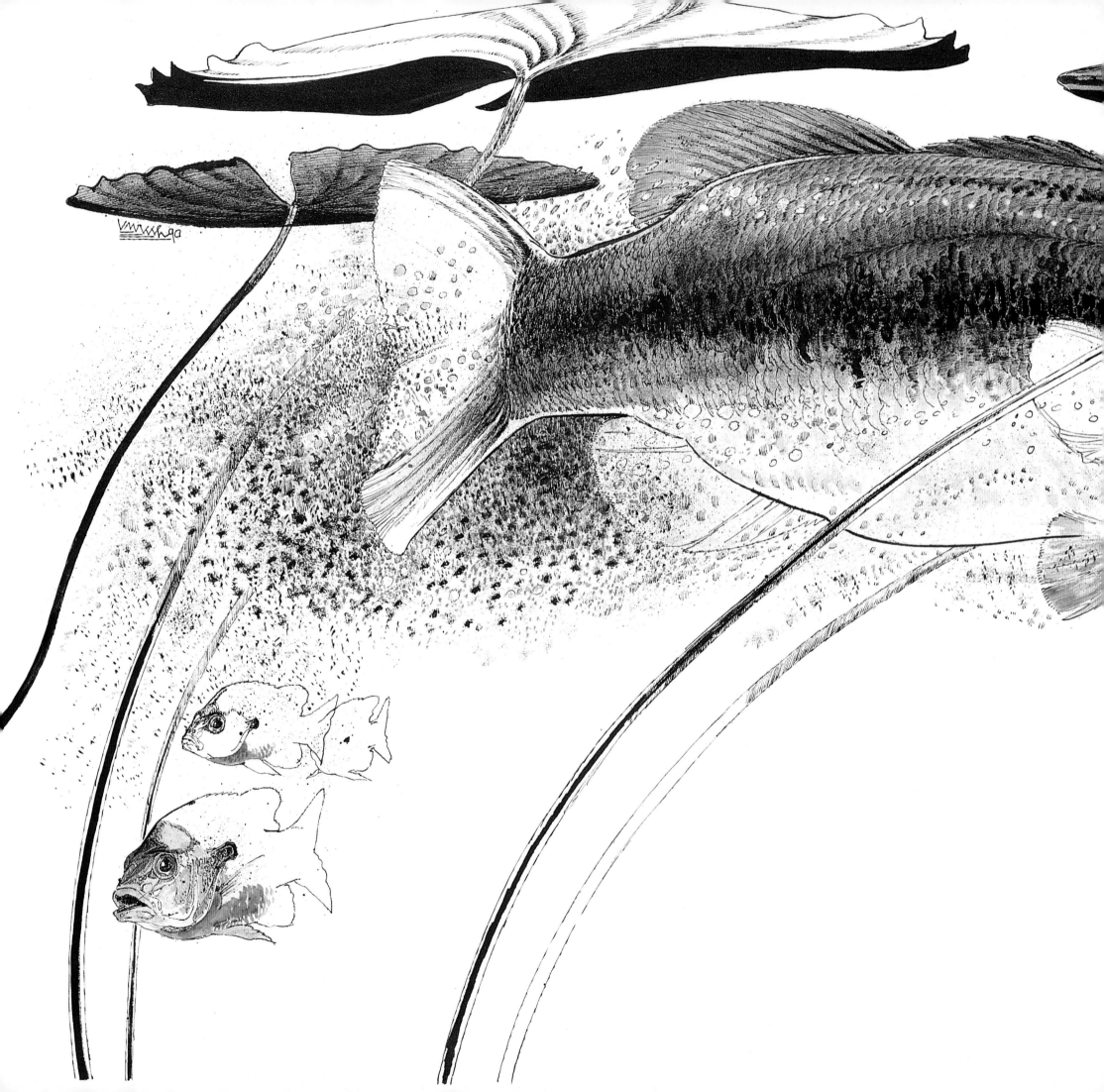

LARGEMOUTH BASS

MICROPTERUS SALMOIDES

Typical weight 2 to 15 pounds

JOHN ALEXANDER

For awhile, John Alexander held the Texas state largemouth record. Then he broke his own record. So he's been the champ twice. John's advice is to fish real slow and deep in the month of February. But when he's driving his boat, he only knows two speeds: flat-out and dead stop. With the small motor—it's rated for 200 horse power—he can hit 72 miles per hour. Decals, patches, endorsements, and gimme hats are all part of his rig—not to mention, his color-coordinated fashionwear.

Illustration by Jack Unruh.

STREAM & SHORE

If levels of enjoyment and dedication do not differentiate bass fishermen, then the relative pace of their fishing may. Shore fishermen, both waders and bank walkers, using all manner of tackle from artful fly rods to functional spincasters, must take the slow road to catching bass. But what a perspective this deliberate approach can provide. While the boat-riding contingent may anticipate yet another spot "down the lake," the wader, or shoreliner, is not burdened with such luxuries. His particular opportunities for success are right in front of him or at least within a few hundred feet in either direction. His measure of satisfaction, then, is just how well he can entice the bass from a relatively limited area.

Among the many methods available, the flyrodder sometimes has a marked advantage over those using "conventional" bass tackle. This is particularly true when using popping bugs or other topwaters for largemouths. In wading a grassy flat during the spring, for instance, the flyrodder is able to make numerous presentations of his bait without ever having to retrieve the line. A spin-fisherman, by comparison, may have an effective lure in a balsawood minnow, but he must reel it in following every cast before he can toss it again. The flyrodder merely picks up the line from the water and redirects the bug.

Of course, the real artists are those flyrodders who stalk smallmouth bass from a river or stream. Not only do they face the challenge of fooling the most wily of the black bass, they must do so in a finicky current, while mending casts and working assorted streamers, bugs, and nymphs. Unlike the static waters of the reservoir or pond, the moving water limits the fisherman's mobility in the pool or run and mutes his sensitivity to strikes. Wading takes special skills and a thoughtful plan of attack. In many ways, these smallmouth chasers are akin to the tournament pros with their selectivity in tackle and attention to detail. Self-contained, flyrodders pack everything that they might use in their vests, but even though they're all dressed up, they really have nowhere to go.

Bank walkers, unlike the tournament crowd, are not subject to any arbitrary rules about techniques or baits. There are seasoned veterans tossing spinnerbaits confidently as they circle a Texas tank. There are adventuresome youths slipping down the face of a steep Kansas pit mine, anxious to toss a live frog into the clear water. And there are those patient Californians, hunched over on a brushy bank, fingering the line as they slowly inch their plastic worms along the bottom. Yet they all share a

Bass-fishing traditions may be traced through the history of bass lures and tackle. George Perry used gear like this to catch the world record in 1932. By Don Wirth.

Shore fishing for bass is a more personal approach, meeting the fish on its own terms. Buffalo River, Tennessee, by Wade Bourne.

certain commonality, a certain collective focus.

If nothing else, shoreline fishing, in its many varieties, puts a premium on the entire experience not just on the predictable cast or obligatory retrieve. Every step to the fishing spot—across a marsh, under barbed wire, along rocky inclines, or over washboard roads—has much to do with màking a memorable fishing trip. Who could recall the difference between one windy boat ride and another? But the shore fisherman can vividly describe snagging a crankbait in the underbrush or nearly losing a boot in the bog. And who could forget the lure hung hopelessly on an underwater snag or the sickening feeling of leaving that last pack of hooks in the trunk of the car?

And what about the elements? While not exactly fair-weather fishermen, most shoreliners are prone to angling during the milder parts of the year. But during the spring, a time when bass have moved toward the shallows (and the shoreliners), the weather forecaster offers no guarantees. High clouds may rapidly give way to thunderheads, and wet and windy times prevail. The boater may quickly escape to the boathouse or duck beneath a bridge. But the bass-fishing shoreliner must make a decision: march back through the wetlands, or hunker down and wait out the storm. More often than not, he stays put and "one more cast" leads to *one more cast.*

And in the end, it is this kind of focus—the undiluted attention of the fisherman on foot—that provides the most exciting bass fishing of all. The sensation of meeting the fish on its own terms, and at close quarters, is unmatched. Bass fishing is not long-distance surf casting, it is far more personal. In fact, it's much more like hunting quail or other upland game birds. Hiding in the brush or weed beds or beneath a pocket of lily pads, the bass is not likely to flush, rather it clings to its hideout. Understanding this trait, 'walkers and waders may move within a few feet of their quarry, able to dangle a plastic worm or a piece of pork rind or even a large nightcrawler, and have the bass strike with abandon.

Surely that is ample reward for the bass-fishing infantry.

SMALLMOUTH BASS
MICROPTERUS DOLOMIEUI
Typical weight 2 to 5 pounds, a good stream fish will be much smaller

Charlie Broad wades wet. He's a fisherman's fisherman—high on technique and skill, low on wardrobe, as attested to by his fancy homemade wading shorts. Charlie grabs the suntan lotion and a few floating bugs (not the kind you need OFF! for—these have rubber legs and wriggle like the lady at the state fair). He loops a stringer to his belt, grabs his fly rod, and another soul is lost, or in this case, a sly smallmouth.

Illustration by Jack Unruh

TAKING IT EASY

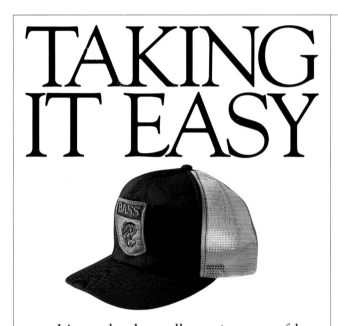

It's not hard to tell certain types of bass fishermen apart. A quick quiz will do. For instance, just ask him to describe a sunrise. If he should respond with something like "It'll be at 5:52 today. They should let us go about 6:30 . . . it'll take me twenty minutes to run to Birney Creek . . ." you know what you've got. A guy going to work—a tournament fisherman. But if his response is filled with awe or appreciation, "Look at that sky, kids!" or "What a way to start the day!" you've found someone (and there are lots of them) who enjoys bass fishing for all it has to offer.

Even without the conversation, you still might recognize this fisherman near the ramp or out on the water. He shows little haste in readying the boat. He loosens one strap and then another, and then he kneels down to check the drain plug. He puts the rods carefully in their places and maybe pauses to tie on a lure. While others bustle in the dim light amid the engine clatter and exhaust, he waits, quietly pondering where he might fish.

His boat, often built of aluminum, may not be the latest model nor is it likely to sport 200 horses on the transom, but you can bet one thing, it's well suited to his kind of fishing—relaxed and comfortable. Swivel seats? Standard equipment. Pedestal seats? If the hull is stable. Carpeting? Put it in himself. Trolling motor? Yep. Third one in 12 years. Sonar? Got to have it. Got to find those drop-offs. He might even carry an anchor or two for when it gets windy. No frills, true. But he's got everything necessary to catch bass, or at least give it a good try.

And he's smart, too. He couldn't beat those big rigs down the lake if he wanted to, so why worry about it? By holding back in the morning, he lets them fire up and spread out, so that when he embarks he can dodge the boat wakes and find his own place to fish. And since the biggest portion of the crowd is already casting when he arrives, his little area is unlikely to be bothered by other boats.

Another type of fisherman takes a different tack for much the same reason. Rather than face another alarm clock morning, he sleeps in, huddles with his family, cleans out the shed, or stops off at the hardware store. There'll be plenty of time after lunch to head out to the lake. What's more, he'll probably miss the typical "midday slump," and if he has things worked out right, he'll miss the tournament crowd set to weigh-in around 3:00. When those guys are

The tackle shop opens early and closes late—plenty of time to go fishing and still bring back a story or two. Central Florida by Lionel Atwill.

done fishing, he'll be heading to quiet waters from now to sunset.

Of course, he doesn't really need the "look-alike" tournament boat. His waters may be much smaller or more placid than the reservoir. Maybe a canoe, with or without an electric motor, or even a float tube or belly boat takes him to his favorite bass hideout. The canoe is ideal for bass bugging on a creek, and the float tube is a stealthful and healthful way of stalking through waters that are not otherwise reachable. But oh, the big bass tales these "tubers" can tell.

"I had this ole sow on and she drug me clean around this cypress log."

Another way to identify the laidback fisherman is to look in his tackle box. It's not in disarray necessarily, but there's a bit less concern for absolute order. You can also immediately recognize his favorite type of fishing. He just can't hide it. If he's a "worm fisherman," all the top trays will be stuffed with plastic crawlers, each by color. Some will be purple, or black, or electric blue, if he's from the old school, or else he'll have salt-and-pepper, or pumpkin, or "cotton candy." And if you look real close, you can even discover his favorites. They're in the tray that's not nearly so full or the one where used worms reveal hook punctures or telltale abrasions made by the bass's bristly teeth.

On the other hand, if the trays open to files of hard plastic baits—chrome and chartreuse and crawfish brown—you know that's what he throws. Crankbaits are popular for numerous reasons. They catch a lot of bass, and they're not nearly as slow and tedious to fish

"No frills" bass fishing never meant "no bass." Farm pond, California, by Mike Jones.

as the plastic worm. Of course, you'll recognize his favorites—those with scratched and faded paint or bent or missing hook points. But he knows what's new. Dig around in the bottom tray and you're sure to find an unopened package containing one of the "hot baits" touted by the pros.

Finding the real experts in the laidback category is easy. Don't look for brand names or mass production lures. The guy who's really dangerous out on the water is the one who makes, carries, and fishes all his own lures. There's no better evidence of a skilled or creative basser than one who has figured out what it takes to catch them—and then builds a cus-tom bait to get the job done. Some anglers mold their own plastic worms or tie jigs with bucktail or other materials. But the most serious ones fashion spoons out of metal, spinnerbaits out of wire and lead, or even carve their own wooden creations. These are the real bassin' men.

Without the fanfare of the high-tech fisherman, the real bassin' man goes about his day enjoying the opportunity to match wits with his favorite fish. He might not know or even recognize world champion Rick Clunn. But he sure knows where there's a 5-pounder snug in a stob out in Birney Creek.

And he may mosey out that way tomorrow.

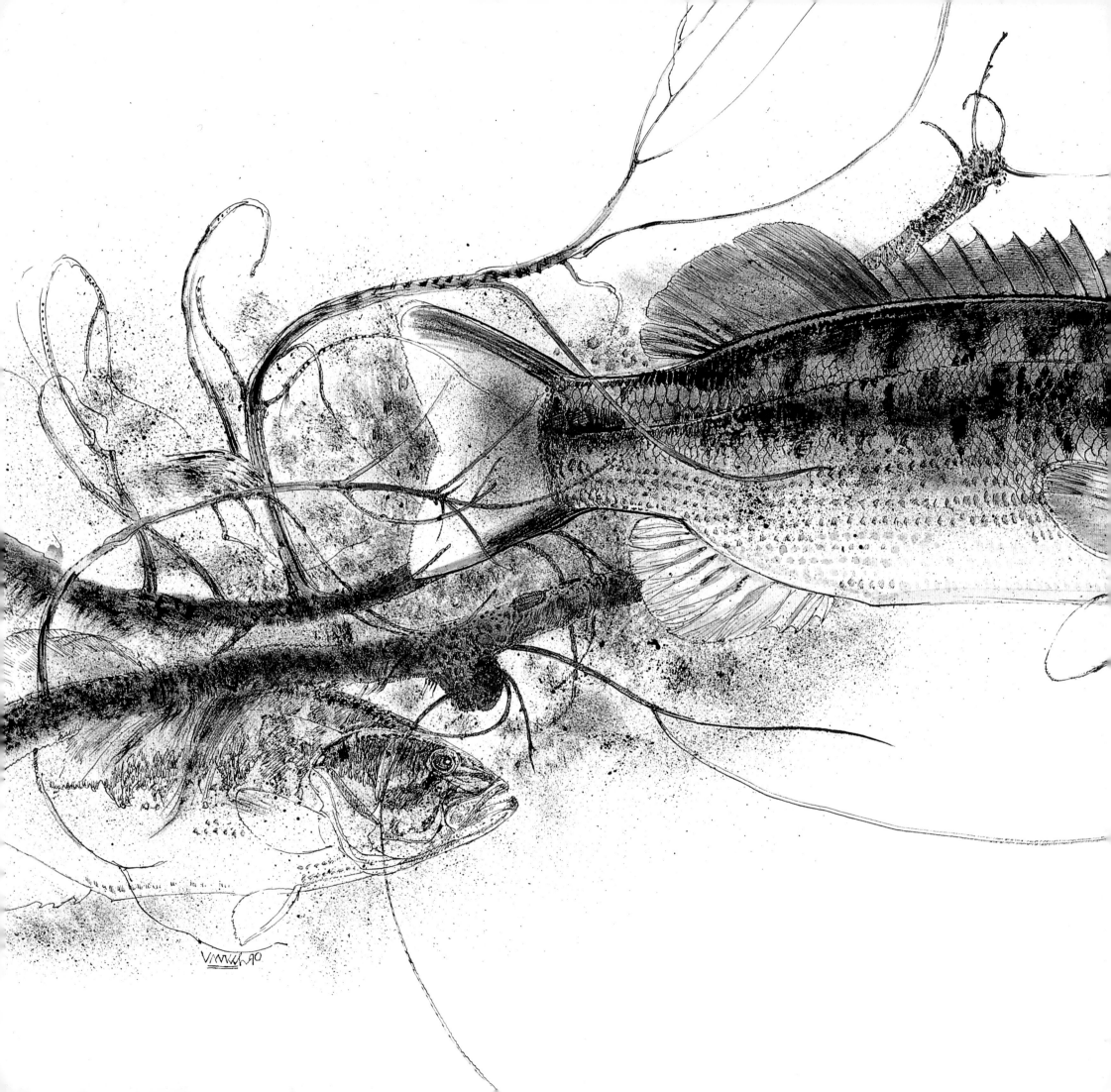

SPOTTED BASS

MICROPTERUS PUNCTULATUS

Typical weight 1 to 4 pounds, a very strong fighter—another characteristic is the teeth on its tongue

MILLeR TIMe

Steve Miller considers himself a pretty fair fisherman when it comes to spotted bass. When the sun starts going down, it's time for him to start working the rocky points. He prefers fishing in the cool of the evening and early in the morning. Nothing fancy for Steve—maybe a can of Vienna sausages, some Fritos, and a few cold ones. Then he deep-fries those little fillets and he's ready to go. Steve says one of the reasons he eats fish is because he gets to eat tartar sauce too. He makes a tolerable sauce.

Illustration by Jack Unruh.

The best part of fishing today is the hope of fishing tomorrow. Lake Griffin, Florida, by Lionel Atwill.

BIBLIOGRAPHY

Bauer, Erwin A. *The Bass Fisherman's Bible*, Rev. ed. Garden City, N.Y.: (Outdoor Bible) Doubleday, 1980.

Bentz, Earl, and Don Wirth. *The Bass Boat Bible*. Nashville: B & W Publications, 1983.

Christian, Chris. *Bass Fishermen's Digest*. Northbrook, Ill.: DBI Books, Inc., 1988.

Gibbs, Jerry. *Bass Myths Exploded*. New York: David McKay Company, Inc., 1978.

Hannon, Douglas and Carter, Horace. *Hannon's Big Bass Magic*. Brainerd, Minn.: In-Fisherman, 1986.

————*Hannon's Field Guide for Bass Fishing*. Odessa, Fla.: D. Hannon, 1983

Hannon, Doug, and Don Wirth. *Catch Bass!* St. Petersburg, Fla.: Great Outdoors Publishing Co., 1984.

Johnson, Paul. *The Scientific Angler*. New York: Charles Scribner's Sons, 1982.

Larsen, Larry. *Bass Fishing Facts*. Lakeland, Fla.: Larsen's Outdoor Publishing, 1989.

————*Bass Lures: Tricks & Techniques*. Lakeland, Fla.: Larsen's Outdoor Publishing, 1988.

————*Bass Pro Strategies*. Lakeland, Fla.: Larsen's Outdoor Publishing, 1988.

————*Shallow Water Bass*. Lakeland, Fla.: Larsen's Outdoor Publishing, 1986.

————. *Follow the Forage for More Bass*. Tabor City, N.C.: Atlantic Publishing Company, 1984.

Lindner, Al, et. al. *Smallmouth Bass: An In-Fisherman Handbook of Strategies*. Brainerd, Minn.: In-Fisherman, 1984.

Martin, Roland. *One Hundred & One Bass-Catching Secrets*. Piscataway, N.J.: New Century Publishers, Inc., 1988.

Meyers, Chet, et. al. *Bass: An In-Fisherman Handbook of Strategies*. Brainerd, Minn.: In-Fisherman, 1981.

Murray, Harry. *Fly Fishing for Smallmouth Bass*. New York: Lyons & Burford Publishers, 1989.

Perry, E. L. "Buck." *Spoonplugging*. Hickory, N.C.: Clay Printing, 1965.

Sisley, Nick. *Bass Magic*. Apollo, Penn.: Nick Sisley, 1984.

Sternberg, Dick. *Smallmouth Bass*. Inglewood Cliffs, N.J.: P-H (Prentice Hall), 1987.

————. *Smallmouth Bass*. Minnetonka, Minn.: Cy De Cosse, 1986.

Taylor, Nick. *Bass Wars*. New York: McGraw-Hill, 1988.

Taylor, Rick. *Guide to Successful Bass Fishing*. Missoula, Mont.: Mountain Press, 1979.

Underwood, Bob A. *Lunker*. New York: McGraw-Hill, 1975.

Whitlock, Dave. *L.L. Bean Fly Fishing for Bass Handbook*. New York: Lyons & Burford Publishers, 1988.

Lake Hodges, California, by Lionel Atwill.

Bass Fishing: An American Tradition was produced in association
with the publisher by McQuiston & Partners in
Del Mar, California: art direction, Don McQuiston;
design, Joyce Sweet; editorial supervision, Tom Chapman and Robin Witkin;
mechanical production, Joyce Sweet and Kristi Paulson Mendola;
copyediting, Robin Witkin; photography not otherwise credited,
John Oldenkamp and Cynthia Sabransky;
illustrations, by Jack Unruh;
composition, TypeLink; text type, Goudy Old Style;
text paper, 157-gsm Glossy Coated; printed in Japan by
Dai Nippon Printing Co., Ltd.